BOOK S ...E'
BEST BOOKS

Celebrating
5
Years!

BO
OK

sense

BOOK SENSE
BEST BOOKS

125 Favorite Books
Recommended by
Independent Booksellers

Compiled by **Book Sense**

Foreword by **Barbara Kingsolver**

Introduction by **Avin Mark Domnitz**

Edited by **Mark Nichols**

NEWMARKET PRESS • NEW YORK

This book is published in the United States of America.

First Edition

10 9 8 7 6 5 4 3 2 1

ISBN 1-55704-643-3

Library of Congress Cataloging-in-Publication Data

Book Sense best books : 125 favorite books recommended by independent booksellers / compiled by Book Sense. —1st ed.
    p. cm.
Includes bibliographical references and index.
ISBN 1-55704-643-3 (pbk. : alk. paper)
    1. Best books—United States. 2. Books and reading—United States. 3. Children—Books and reading—United States. I. Book Sense (Program)
    Z1035.B715 2005
    011'.73—dc22

                                    2004019467

QUANTITY PURCHASES

Companies, professional groups, clubs, and other organizations may qualify for special terms when ordering quantities of this title. For information, write Special Sales Department, NEWMARKET PRESS, 18 EAST 48TH STREET, NEW YORK, NY 10017; call (212) 832-3575; FAX (212) 832-3629; or e-mail mailbox@newmarketpress.com.

www.newmarketpress.com

Designed by Kevin McGuinness

Manufactured in the United States of America.

✄ CONTENTS

Foreword

MARKING A PASSAGE
❧ BARBARA KINGSOLVER

IN 1958, WHEN I WAS HARDLY YET A DOT ON ANY MAP, A NEW
bookstore opened its doors at the eastern end of the main
street of what would one day become my hometown,
Tucson, Arizona. The bookstore filled its shelves, and customers happily bought what was there, then asked for more,
until the Book Mark came to assume the higgledy-piggledy
atmosphere I associate with old London bookshops: high
bookshelves stacked even higher on top with oversize stock
lying sideways; sliding ladders shoved up and down narrow
aisles crammed with every kind of wisdom. And always, of
course, the friendly staff waiting to help track it down. One
of them was a tiny woman named Anne whose memory pre-
saged computers. She could identify just about anything ever
published, declare it in stock, and scramble up a ladder for

it, hanging up there near the ceiling fixtures and chattering away about what *else* the author had written, while your heart quailed lest she fall and dash her frail bones.

Twenty-five years later, when I was still on nobody's map but my own, I had claimed that marvelous bookstore as my territory: I met friends there, attended my first literary readings, gained a little confidence at debating art and politics, gave and received recommendations for the obscure but spectacular first novel that would have to be read before anyone's life went one step farther. Once in this bookish meeting place I even began a star-crossed love affair behind the discreetly turned spines of Virginia Woolf and Leo Tolstoy.

And then came the year 1988, when, unbelievably (to me, anyway), I was about to publish an obscure first novel of my own. My New York publisher turned out a few thousand copies, and we all hoped most of them would sell before it faded out of print. This is the way of first novels, which aren't generally greeted with trumpets. Mostly they are greeted with yawns. That is why most writers starve, or else have day jobs.

I was lucky though. I had a guardian angel, a tiny one named Anne, who loved my book and made it her mission to shove it into the hands of everyone she thought would like it. This meant pretty much every unarmed human being who entered the Book Mark, and some who were merely hanging around in the parking lot. I had other guardian angels, too, it turns out: booksellers all over the country who discovered my novel and sold it "by hand" as they say in the business.

Booksellers proceeded to change my life, and they have changed it since then in some ways they've probably never imagined. My name, for instance, used to be a disaster that nobody could spell. You don't just blurt out a name like mine, because it leaves people breathless and staring as if you'd made an inappropriate noise. For about thirty years I never said my name without spelling it: "Kingsolver — K-I-N-G-S as in Sam-O-L-V as in Victor-E-R—yes, ma'am, just like it sounds." That's twenty-six syllables. I still have to do that sometimes, but not at the library, no indeed, and not when I call to place an order at a bookstore. "Kingsolver, like the author?" they'll ask. "Any relation?" And I'll say yes, I think so. If I'm feeling sassy I'll say, "Yes, I'm married to her husband." How can I measure what this means in my life, to have a last name that's been reduced from twenty-six syllables to three?

And that's nothing at all compared with the joy of working at a job I love. I'm finally pretty confident that I have quit the last of the long string of day jobs I held for so many years to support my writing, and now—thirteen years later—I don't think any of my old bosses is expecting me back. Each day as I sit down to work on writing a book, I begin by laying my hands gently across my keyboard and offering up my silent thanks to readers, to the people who publish books, and to the people who sell them—the people without whom I would not get to do what I do.

When my first novel came out in its three- or four-thousand-copy edition, my publisher and I crossed our fingers for luck, because that's how it is for little first novels with funny names on their spines that nobody can spell. After my guardian angels began to press it into people's hands, it went back to print, then back to print again, and while it didn't break any records for a first novel, it got read, all over the place. I earned enough royalties so I didn't have to go back to my day job to feed my baby and keep up with the mortgage. Instead, I got to stay at my desk and write a second book, then a third and a fourth. I finished each one with the help of booksellers who were rooting for my career. Now the copies of my books out in the world number in many millions, a lot of them in languages I can't read. This strikes me as a miracle on the order of the loaves and fishes.

Ten years after that first precarious launch of a first novel, my friends at the Book Mark asked me to give the debut reading of my eighth book, *The Poisonwood Bible*, at their store, and I told them I couldn't imagine any better place to launch it. I stood on a raised platform in their parking lot, surrounded by hundreds of cheering Tucsonans, and felt a little like Eva Peron. I swore I would never forget that day or the people there who had first guided readers to my words, and to whom I know, absolutely, I owed my career. I thought of them as family. When my second daughter was born I sent them a birth announcement, which they proudly displayed.

Then, the February following that marvelous coronation in their parking lot, they sent me a much less joyful announcement: After forty years, the Book Mark was passing away. Tucsonans' buying habits were changing, it seemed. They were purchasing through the Internet, hunting for bargains, and drawn by the lure of chain stores.

Over the next weeks I determined to go in often to say goodbye to my favorite aisles and buy more books from their emptying shelves. The store had to sell as much of its stock as it could, I realized, but I dreaded that on my visits I would feel as if I were sifting through the goods of a dying relative. Nevertheless, I made myself march down to my bookstore with the same cheer and courage that my old friend Anne, now deceased, had once brought to the project of hand-selling my first novel. I hugged each of my friends behind the counter and told them: I can't bear this passing.

I couldn't, and still can't, because the scene is repeating itself in cities everywhere as other small and large independents announce their final closing sales. I'm grateful, of course, that books are still sold elsewhere, in other stores including the national chains, and I know that in some small towns that have never before had the privilege of having a real bookstore, the nationally run stores now turning up may be a godsend. I appreciate the reading series and book clubs they have organized where such things have never happened before. The big stores have their place; I'd just be happiest if it weren't *in place of* the other kind. I have a bone to pick with any behemoth if its strategy includes purposefully locating close to, and out-competing, the neighborhood shops by offering discounts on its most popular stock. I am uncomfortable with taking advantage of a bargain if the store's size allowed it to snag that book for a reduced price from a publisher that didn't offer the same deal to the independents. (Independent booksellers have challenged this practice in court.) Publishers also subsidize certain books by giving "co-op money" to all booksellers; the chains get these subsidies on a scale that determines which books will move forward into the large, front-of-the-store displays. This practice means that people in many cities at once will hardly be able to walk in the door of their nearest big bookstore without tripping over a stack of the new Stephen King or—yes—the latest Barbara Kingsolver.

I am stunned and flattered to find myself so prominently displayed, and deeply grateful for support I've received from any and all bookselling quarters. But I'm humbled by what I know of my roots: I wasn't always up there, front and center. Once I was the name no one could spell, on the spine of a book that could have gone quietly out of print while its author went back to freelance science writing or professional (but cheerless) housecleaning. There but for the grace of my guardian angels go I. If I were trying to launch a writing career today, I would be launching it into very different waters. I could not possibly have as much support from independent booksellers as I did back then, simply because there are not as many of them now. I'd be taking more of my chances in the chains, as an impossible name on the spine of a little lost book somewhere in the back of the store—a needle in a brightly lit haystack. I can't be sure I'd be a writer today if that's what I was up against, starting out. What I'm sure of is this: Mine would have been much more of an uphill struggle without my legions of bookseller-promoters, and I would not have been able to write as many books. Some of the titles I've given the world would not be in it. There would be no glorious launching of *The Poisonwood Bible* in the parking lot of the Book Mark; there would be no Book Mark, and no *Poisonwood Bible*. I don't like this grim re-visioning of my life as it might have been, but it's the truth.

It's not only starving artists who should care about what we're losing when an independent bookstore dies. This is not about retail; it's about people who serve as community organizers in places where you can always find kindred spirits, a good read, maybe even love behind the spine of Virginia Woolf. A store where you can be sure no one will say to you, as happened to someone I know when he went into a place I shall not name, asking for *Catcher in the Rye*: "Um, check the sports aisle?"

Putting an extra dollar or two back into our hometown's economy, rather than sending it off to a distant, faceless conglomerate, is worth what it costs for so many reasons. Holding on to our independent booksellers is nothing less than a First Amendment issue. To put it bluntly, megasellers and megapublishers have significant power, when put together, to manipulate what Americans will see, purchase, and read. Their power has its purpose, but it needs to be balanced. "Independent" means what it says: stores that are locally owned, by people who know books and need not tailor their orders to the appetites of a distant city, but would rather honor their customers' interests in regional issues, local authors, small-press books, poetry, first novels—things that matter to *us*, right here, right now. Is this something you can live without?

Apparently, the answer for lots of us is that yes, we can, and we will have to. Miraculously, Tucson still has a glorious feminist independent named Antigone Books that's still going strong after more than twenty years, as well as a raft of specialty and used bookstores. But most of the rest have gone the way of Arizona's native fish: One by one their streams dried up, and they went extinct. Wonderful names—the Haunted Bookshop, Coyote's Voice, Marco Polo, Whiz Kids—are now a kind of secret code that passes poignantly between old-time Tucsonans who love to read. And now another has joined them—that bookish trout that swam upstream for so long, the Book Mark.

For those sad last weeks of its closing sale I was stuck in the earliest stage of grief: denial. I kept banking on a miracle on the order of Jimmy Stewart's in *It's a Wonderful Life*. People would show up there in droves with cash in hand, I thought, to prove that their hearts had not been sold after all for the three-dollar markdown. The prodigal readers would return, and those who had never left would also come back to scour the aisles, looking for the enlightenment and passions and how-to manuals that filled our lives before TV stultified and bumfuz-zled us. And this actually did happen, in a way: People came in to the store begging to know how they could help, even offer-ing to invest their savings. But for that store, it was too late.

I keep running across the phrase "because of the demise of the independent bookstore," and it causes me to get hot under the collar. The reports of this death are greatly exaggerated—I just can't believe the independents will all go down. The tides of fortune will reverse themselves, I still tell myself, every time I read of another closure. It will happen because this is America, where we love to believe in our own story, the possi-bility that any one of us could write the Great American Novel, and the rest of us could read it, without waiting for Big Brother to buy it a place at the table. It will happen because we're devoted, above all, to independence and freedom of thought.

Aren't we?

Introduction

GOOD ADVICE FROM PEOPLE YOU TRUST
 AVIN MARK DOMNITZ

CONVENTIONAL WISDOM IS A POWERFUL FORCE. OUR VIEW OF
the world is often shaped by ideas we *believe* to be true. When
I entered bookselling in 1979, I was thrilled by the notion that
it was a nice little business existing in its own corner of the
world, exempt from the pressures of retail in general. Well...
so much for conventional wisdom.

The 1980s and 1990s brought a massive influx of capital to
fuel an unprecedented expansion in bookselling, initially by
mall-based chain stores, then by large "super-stores," and ultimately, "big box" mass merchandisers. Suddenly our nice little
business was transformed into late twentieth-century retail.
Public ownership changed a love of letters into a reverence for
the bottom line. Somewhere amidst the conversations about
return on investment, retail distribution centers, commodity
publishing, huge advances that had to be "earned out," and the
concept of "buying" shelf space for in-store displays, an ideal
was lost.

Independent booksellers have always had a deep appreciation for what 2004 *Publishers Weekly* Bookseller of the Year A. David Schwartz described as "the soul of the book." The idea that every book was the physical manifestation of the product of one human mind and was to be revered was central to the concept of the book as something other than a commodity. Although their number were shrinking in the nineties, independent booksellers doggedly served their local communities and unflaggingly continued to dispense good advice to the millions of readers who trusted them. They continued to create bookstores that were, in effect, that "Great, Good Place" specifically fashioned to the uniqueness of the communities that they served.

In spite of this, independents had a huge problem. Nowhere was there a repository for their aggregate knowledge, taste, and sensibilities regarding notable books. Indeed, some booksellers believed that gathering and harnessing the power and knowledge of this truly independent group of souls to be anathema to the very concept of "independence." Ultimately, the problem was how to create a national marketing program and a consumer brand that could convey the key facets of the independent bookstore identity without losing the essence that makes independent booksellers unique and great... their diversity... their differences.

In 1998, the Board of Directors of the Northern California Independent Booksellers Association (NCIBA), with the help of the Addison Group, a prominent national marketing firm, wrestled with the problem. Their solution was nothing short of brilliant. Don't brand the sameness... brand the difference. Independent booksellers possess a common set of attributes, but all exhibit these attributes in their own way. They all have knowledge, passion, character, community, and personality, but each shows those attributes in a different, unique, and independent way.

And thus Book Sense was born. Knowing that the key challenges facing Northern California booksellers were no different than those of other independents around the country, the NCIBA magnanimously turned over the implementation of Book Sense to the American Booksellers Association.

In 1999, the Book Sense Marketing program for storefront, independent booksellers was launched. It consists of four main components. The Book Sense Bestsellers List is the most current report of what's actually selling in independent bookstores around the country. The Book Sense Gift Certificate Program (now an electronic Gift Card Program) allows customers in any part of the country to buy a gift certificate in an independent bookstore and have it used by the recipient in another part of the country. (This simple act was only possible in chain bookstores until the advent of the Book Sense Program.) The third component is a national Internet presence for independent storefront retailers called BookSense.com, which allows independent retailers to meet the needs of their customers 24/7.

Finally, there is the real cornerstone of the Book Sense program, the Book Sense Picks List, which harnesses what independent booksellers do best...recommend books, one book at a time. Almost every independent bookshop has a "staff recommends" section in which booksellers with impeccable taste and an intimate knowledge of their customers' reading habits share their credibility and expertise, suggesting books to their customers that they think are important for any number of reasons. They may be excellent in a literary sense, or a political sense, or an environmental sense, or a psychological sense, or they may just tell a great story. In the Book Sense Picks program, the compilation of those recommendations, a pantheon of great books and great ideas, has been created.

The sustenance of a free society is a marketplace of ideas that is unfettered by the constraints of government or purchasing power. Democracy dies behind closed doors. The Book Sense Picks program throws open the doors to thoughts and ideas by bringing together a selection of books having only one rule concerning their selection... they were recommended by booksellers working in the more than 1,200 Book Sense bookstores around the country. For these titles, diversity is their hallmark and excellence is their common thread.

Five years have passed swiftly. There have been thirty-two lists of titles picked by independents (not to mention numerous "specialty lists" as well), featuring thousands of recommendations. From the 223 titles comprising the "Top Ten" adult books and 152 titles making up the "Top Ten" children's books from the first five years, independent booksellers have chosen the *Best of the First Five Years of Book Sense*. We present them to you here with full confidence of their quality. We are pleased to provide recommendations from our bookseller members for reading groups and a section of children's and young adults' classics. They are, after all, good advice from people you trust. They are from Book Sense bookstores...independent bookstores for people with independent minds.

❦ THE TOP PICKS

ON THE OCCASION OF THE FIFTH ANNIVERSARY OF THE BOOK Sense program, more than 1,200 participating booksellers were asked to choose those books—both adult and children's titles—which they most enjoyed "handselling" during the first five years of the program.

After receiving ballots from hundreds and hundreds of individual booksellers, the twenty-five books featured in the following pages—fifteen adult titles, comprised of ten fiction and five nonfiction books, and ten children's titles—have been designated as the Book Sense Best Books of the First Five Years, and are presented in alphabetical order. These are the "New Classics," destined to have a long and active life on both bookstore and consumer shelves, picked by independent booksellers as tried and true reader favorites. As you read the recommendations for these titles, you can sense each of the attributes of a Book Sense bookseller—personality, passion, knowledge, community, and character—and you can trust that these books are worthy of your attention.

Adult Fiction

ATONEMENT

❧ BY IAN MCEWAN

"McEwan weaves an absorbing tale that starts one afternoon in 1935 and unfolds for years to come, profoundly altering the lives of those involved. Readers are captivated by a tale that commands attention from start to finish. A beautifully written and masterfully crafted tale of growing up, finding love, and the dangers of a runaway imagination."

—**Kyle Beachy**, *Verbatim Booksellers,*
Vail, CO

"Already a Booker winner, McEwan's writing has only improved. Majestic sentences, palpable characters, and an utterly engrossing plot serve to make this novel of love, family, betrayal, and redemption at once thoroughly evocative of its time, and a timeless classic."

—**Candler Hunt**, *Olsson's Books & Records,*
Washington DC

BEL CANTO

BY ANN PATCHETT

"A beautiful narrative, seamlessly written about a hostage situation in Latin America with an international cast, including an American opera singer, a Japanese businessman, a native priest, the terrorists, and the fascinating translator Gen, who enables them all to communicate with each other. Fierce discussion can be had over the characters' behavior in this stressful situation, the liaisons made, and most of all the twist at the end."

—**Deb Wehemeir**, *Garden District Book Shop,*
New Orleans, LA

"I could not put this marvelous book down. Patchett has based her new novel on a true event—the hostage situation in Peru a few years back—but, boy, does she put a new twist on the story. I won't reveal what happens; please read this book for yourself!"

—**Roberta Rubin**, *The Book Stall at Chestnut Court,*
Winnetka, IL

THE DA VINCI CODE
BY DAN BROWN

"*The Da Vinci Code* astounds the reader with the precision of detail: Dan Brown has researched each aspect of the secret society, architecture, and symbology used in the storyline. While it is possible to draw one's own conclusions from the facts, these buildings—artworks and societies do exist as described in the book—allow those who enjoy follow-up research to have even more fun!"

—**Scott Werbin**, *The Tudor Bookshop*,
Kingston, PA

"Everyone here has read and loved this smart new thriller. This is one of those rare books that comes along and makes you question everything you thought you knew about religion, art, and what you were taught in school. It's fast-paced, enthralling, and simply impossible to put down."

—**Jeff Azbill**, *Davis-Kidd Booksellers*,
Jackson, TN

EMPIRE FALLS
BY RICHARD RUSSO

"With *Empire Falls* Richard Russo once again delivers the goods and, in so doing, further establishes himself as one of the country's most accomplished writers. Certainly there is no better portrayer of small-town life and its everyday sinners and small saints, as opposed to the ironic tyros and sly heroes who mar much of recent fiction. Empire Falls, the town titling the book, contains stories of family and failed ambition, of the past intruding upon the present, tragedy both horrible and comic, and, finally, a believable, if ambiguous hope in a future beyond the town."

—John Teague, *Politics and Prose Books and Coffee*
Washington, DC

"Russo draws us into the life of a man for whom everything seems settled but now is suddenly quite unsettled. As events unfold, Russo's depiction of this small town and those who are shaped by it is so lifelike you will find yourself revisiting them long after you finish the book. This tale is ribald, melancholy, and nearly perfect. Russo is a master of the intricacies of everyday lives."

—Jean Westcott, *Olsson's Books & Records,*
Arlington, VA

LIFE OF PI

BY YANN MARTEL

"*Life of Pi* is an incredible prize on my bookshelf. Yann Martel completely took me into the full, brilliant world of his storytelling in which Pi Patel is shipwrecked and shares a raft with a Bengal tiger. This novel defies easy classification as an "adventure" novel, however. It shows how the real is fantastical and how the fantastical can be real. It was engrossing, witty, thoroughly enjoyable, and inspiring to the imagination and to the soul."

—Janet Blackwood, *Town Book Store*,
Westfield, NJ

"Martel weaves a brilliant tale that is part adventure story and part spiritual quest. The part of the book that relates how Pi becomes a practicing Hindu/Moslem/Christian is worth the price of the book, and the portion that deals with Pi and a Bengal tiger adrift on the ocean in a lifeboat together is everything you might imagine and more."

—Stephen Grutzmacher, *Passtimes Books*,
Sister Bay, WI

THE LOVELY BONES
BY ALICE SEBOLD

"The narrator of this extraordinary novel is Susie Salmon, recently murdered and new to heaven. Susie watches her family and friends cope with the shock and grief of her death and tracks the movements of the investigation into her murder. We are riveted by the movements of her murderer, enthralled by Susie's heaven, and heartened by her touching examination of her love of her family and her sadness at how her death has torn them apart. A wonderful story."
> —Barbara Hoagland, *The King's English,*
> Salt Lake City, UT

"An original, touching story of a murder and the aftermath narrated in the wry, often humorous voice of the teenage victim as she watches the events unfold from her own version of heaven."
> —Erin O'Donnell, *Seattle Mystery Bookshop,*
> Seattle, WA

PEACE LIKE A RIVER

✦ BY LEIF ENGER

"*Peace Like a River* is the most unique and impressive novel that I have read in a long time. With a strong narrative voice, creative story, and detailed, exquisite characterization, this book just flows. Enger's writing is so good that I often found myself stopping to re-read lines, (or to read them to my friends!). At the end, I had a difficult time separating myself from the characters and the wonderful adventures that we had together. *Peace Like a River* is the special sort of book that doesn't come along every day. Read it, and savor it."

—Jen Reynolds, *Joseph-Beth and Davis-Kidd Booksellers,*
Cincinnati, OH

"What a book! I was captivated from page one. His pitch-perfect prose is a pleasure to read, and his imaginative storytelling took me through the whole range of human emotion. *Peace Like a River* deserves a huge audience, it's that good."

—Mark LaFramboise, *Politics and Prose Books and Coffee,*
Washington, DC

THE POISONWOOD BIBLE
BY BARBARA KINGSOLVER

"*Poisonwood Bible* is on my lifetime top-ten-favorite-books list. As I read the first sentences I almost shivered with excitement. Kingsolver's incredible descriptive language had me transfixed and I knew immediately I was going to love this book!"
>   —Linda Glass, *Bohannons' Books with a Past,*
>   Georgetown, KY

"This is Kingsolver's richest, most complex, and most deeply affecting novel yet. It offers the reader so much on so many levels."
>   —Amy McCurdy, *DIESEL: A Bookstore,*
>   Oakland, CA

"A fascinating novel about the politics and culture of the Belgian Congo in the late 1950s. The story is told by the wife and four daughters of Nathan Price, an evangelical Baptist missionary. The family is transformed during their three decades in postcolonial Africa."
>   —Wilfried & Lilo Eder, *Fort Ashby Books,*
>   Fort Ashby, WV

THE RED TENT
*≈ BY ANITA DIAMANT

"Wow! Quite simply, one of the best books I've ever read. You will never look at history, the Bible, or your relationship with your mother the same way again. Compelling and moving, *The Red Tent* is a truly awesome book. (Fans of *The Bonesetter's Daughter* [by Amy Tan], here's one you should really read for the mother/daughter connection!)"

—**Megan Scott O'Bryan**, *Scott's Bookstore*,
Mount Vernon, WA

"A powerful retelling of the biblical story of Dinah, told from a feminist perspective."

—**Miriam Sontz**, *Powell's*,
Portland OR

"*The Red Tent* offers something for readers of all ages and backgrounds. History, bible lore, relationships between women and between family members are all presented while exploring the strong role that women played in ancient times. A very powerful and moving book."

—**Susan Danner**, *Danner's Books & Coffee Shop*,
Muncie, IN

THE SECRET LIFE OF BEES

BY SUE MONK KIDD

"Set in the racially charged climate of South Carolina in the mid-1960s, *The Secret Life of Bees* is the amazing story of a girl's search for her mother. Fleeing an abusive father and the police, Lily and her black "nanny" Rosaleen leave their homes and end up in the world of the "Calendar Sisters"— May, June, and August. This moving book deals with difficult race and family issues in a very refreshing way, and you will fall in love with the eccentric cast of characters."

—Heather Drury, *Hawley-Cooke Booksellers*,
Louisville, KY

"Kidd creates a narrator whom the reader will grow to love. White, fourteen, and a runaway, she finds the true meaning of family in a very unusual place: the home of three black sisters who raise bees. Beautifully written, this is a page-turner."

—Kathy Westover, *The Bookworm*,
Edwards, CO

Adult Nonfiction

DEVIL IN THE WHITE CITY
MURDER, MAGIC, AND
MADNESS AT THE FAIR
THAT CHANGED AMERICA
⁂ BY ERIK LARSON

"Larson's depiction of the creation of the 1893 Chicago
World's Fair and the concurrent story of the serial killer H.H.
Holmes, who stalked Chicago during the same period, is so
fascinating, spellbinding, and even spine-tingling that I can
guarantee you will have a hard time putting it down. Larson
has crafted a portrait of evil that readers won't soon forget."
—**Vincent Desjardins**, *The Snow Goose Bookstore,*
Stanwood, WA

"A must-read that vividly portrays the last grand gasp of the
nineteenth century—the Chicago World's Fair of 1893. Henry
Holmes is the titular devil, a charismatic young doctor with
bloodcurdling obsessions. The supporting cast includes such
luminaries as Edison, Buffalo Bill, and Susan B. Anthony.
Larson fully engulfs the reader in the period, and the enjoyment
is only heightened by the knowledge that the story is true."
—**Scott Coffman**, *Hawley-Cooke Booksellers,*
Louisville, KY

DON'T LET'S GO TO THE DOGS TONIGHT
AN AFRICAN CHILDHOOD
BY ALEXANDRA FULLER

"Told in the irrepressible voice of a young white African girl growing up during the Rhodesian civil war, this memoir is a mixture of joy, tragedy, and reality. While her parents are fighting for what they consider to be justifiable control over the black population, the author is experiencing an unforgettable childhood. As amazing as it is to witness history through her eyes, it was the last line that seemed most timely: 'It's Life carrying on. It's the next breath we all take. It's the choice we make to get on with it.'"

—**Connie Heppner**, *Full Circle Bookstore,*
Oklahoma City, OK

"Here's a fascinating story of growing up in Rhodesia with eccentric parents passionately committed to a white presence in Africa. Things go badly, but Fuller tells of the beginning of Zimbabwe and her family's moves to Malawi and Zambia with both humor and poignancy."

—**Marcia Rider**, *Capitola Book Café,*
Capitola, CA

FAST FOOD NATION
THE DARK SIDE OF THE ALL-AMERICAN MEAL
BY ERIC SCHLOSSER

"The fast food industry has become synonymous with American culture: a delicious package filled with enough flavor-enhanced goodness that, once eaten as a child, hooks customers for life—a corporate beast creating PR blinders to disguise its low wages, its disregard for unsafe working conditions, and the communities that it bleeds for labor and profit. Schlosser dissects every facet of the industry, creating a long overdue work that stands with Sinclair's *The Jungle* as an exposé of American corporate blight."

—**Cleve Corner**, *Politics and Prose Books and Coffee,*
Washington, DC

"This is shocking, comprehensive, and carefully reasoned, and it explains how the fast food industry impacts our health, our culture, our land, and the people who work it. It is an important book and has changed me completely."

—**Kay Marcotte**, *Page One Books,*
Albuquerque, NM

NICKEL AND DIMED
ON (NOT) GETTING BY IN AMERICA
BY BARBARA EHRENREICH

"Feminist, social critic, and journalist Barbara Ehrenreich travels across the U.S. and tries to live off the wages of a waitress, a hotel maid, a Wal-Mart sales clerk, and more to see the reality of what the majority of people in the United States have to deal with. She finds out how mentally and physically skilled one has to be to have these so-called 'unskilled' jobs, and how much intelligence and tenacity you need to survive. Her journalistic style, interlaced with her passion and quick wit, make it an engaging and powerful read."

—Tova Stabin, *Mother Kali's Books,*
Eugene, OR

"Whatever financial woes the middle class may have, they pale in comparison to the daily breadwinning struggle of America's low wage workers. We expect the dirty work to be done, and Ehrenreich gives us a glimpse into the lives of the people who do it. An important work."

—Dan Schreffler, *The Book House of Stuyvesant Plaza,*
Albany, NY

SEABISCUIT
AN AMERICAN LEGEND
BY LAURA HILLENBRAND

"I had never heard of Seabiscuit until I picked up this book, but Laura Hillenbrand has brought this unlikely champion racehorse and the men who owned, trained, and rode him to vivid life. You don't have to be a horse lover to enjoy this book—it is as much a portrait of America during the Depression or a tale of ordinary individuals succeeding against all odds as it is a horse story. This is a captivating, page-turning story of three men and a horse who captured the attention of the entire world."

—**Laura Hudson**, *The Bookloft*,
Great Barrington, MA

"Hillenbrand gifts us with an incredible history of a time, a place, and an entire culture. Like other great books about a storm, a ship, an adventure, the legendary racehorse is a wonderful inspiration for Hillenbrand's larger story...though even if it were just the horse, it would be enough. A great adventure told by a writer worthy of the task."

—**Laura Snyder**, *Lucy's Books*,
Astoria, OR

Children's

THE BAD BEGINNING
A SERIES OF UNFORTUNATE EVENTS, BOOK I
❧ BY LEMONY SNICKET

"Move over, Murphy! Lemony Snicket is the new king of calamity. Whatever can go wrong, will, when this depressingly gifted raconteur takes pen in hand and recites the woes of the Baudelaire orphans. Young Violet (an inventor), Klaus (a reader), and baby Sunny (a biter) thought life could get no worse, but with every new book, it most assuredly does. In order to grow up and collect their trust fund, they must survive the predations of the greedy Count Olaf, incompetent guardians, and an endless number of bad puns. These books rival those of Roald Dahl with their witty word-play and morosely hilarious sensibility. We're hooked!"

—Jenny Lawton, *Just Books,*
Greenwich, CT

"This is Hitchcock/Gorey for a younger generation. The mysterious Snicket has created a fascinating series [in which] there is more here than meets the eye!"

—Kathleen Mahinske, *Book Connection,*
Livonia, MI

BECAUSE OF WINN-DIXIE

BY KATE DICAMILLO

"I can't say it better than Karen Hesse did: 'Take one disarmingly engaging protagonist and put her in the company of a tenderly rendered canine, and you've got yourself a recipe for the best kind of down-home literary treat. Kate DiCamillo's voice in *Because of Winn-Dixie* should carry from the steamy, sultry pockets of Florida clear across the miles to enchant young readers everywhere.' Winner of the 2000 Newbery Honor Award."

—**Michael Barnard**, *Rakestraw Books*, Danville, CA

"India Opal is one of the strongest, most sensitive, and sensible heroines since Scout in *To Kill a Mockingbird*. Kate DiCamillo's first novel is a marvel. Not to be missed!"

—**Collette Morgan**, *Wild Rumpus*, Minneapolis, MN

DEAR MRS. LARUE
LETTERS FROM OBEDIENCE SCHOOL
BY MARK TEAGUE

"I love Mark Teague's work, and his latest is as much for the little ones as for us who will be reading it to them. Ike, as you will see, is a rather untrustworthy narrator. Having been sent to obedience school—an unjustified banishment as far as he is concerned—the terrier writes letters home. Ingeniously Teague shows Ike up by contrasting black-and-white and color depictions of what Ike writes home about and of reality."

—Sara Colglazier, *The Odyssey Bookshop,*
South Hadley, MA

"What a witty book! Little dog Ike has been sent to obedience school by his owner, and his letters home make it sound like a prison. But the funny illustrations show us otherwise."

—Kara Luger, *Chinook Bookshop,*
Colorado Springs, CO

DIARY OF A WORM

BY DOREEN CRONIN
ILLUSTRATED BY HARRY BLISS

"The world from a worm's point of view will tickle the funny bone of the picture book generation. Teachers will love sharing this book and using it as an incentive for young writers. A perfect introduction to journal writing."

—**Judy Hamel**, *Children's Corner Bookshop*,
Spokane, WA

"A favorite author comes up with another big family hit. Would you believe a precocious worm who keeps a diary documenting his life discoveries?"

—**Elsie Peterson**, *The Cottage Book Shop*,
Glen Arbor, MI

"I have read this a countless number of times with my five-year-old daughter and still enjoy it every time. There are laughs for every age group in this one!"

—**Jane Phalen**, *Books, Etc*,
Guttenberg, IA

ERAGON
INHERITANCE, BOOK I
BY CHRISTOPHER PAOLINI

"Take one young man unexpectedly thrust into a life
of legendary fame, evil rulers, giants, and other foes too
incredible to name, a wizened mentor, an assortment of
dwarves and elves, stir in a touch of mystery, magic, and
heroic deeds and you have just a taste of the delights awaiting
you in *Eragon*. Try to keep your breath as you soar through
the air on the back of Saphira, Eragon's loving, gentle, fierce
dragon as he takes on all those who intend evil. *Eragon*, the
stunning first novel by nineteen-year-old Christopher Paolini,
leaves me eagerly awaiting the sequel."

—**Marilyn Smith**, *Hawley-Cooke Booksellers*,
Louisville, KY

"*Eragon* is a guaranteed hit for any reader who loves
fantasy. Drawing on the tradition of J. R. R. Tolkien, Anne
McCaffrey, Ursula K. Le Guin, Philip Pullman, and other
great fantasists, Christopher Paolini has woven together an
exciting suspense-filled adventure of one young man coming
of age in partnership with the first dragon born in over a
century. I can't wait to read the rest of the trilogy."

—**Peter Glassman**, *Books of Wonder*,
New York, NY

THE GOLDEN COMPASS
HIS DARK MATERIALS, BOOK I
~ BY PHILIP PULLMAN

"In *The Golden Compass*, Pullman introduces his readers to Lyra, a head-strong girl with an all-important destiny and an ever-present desire to explore the world beyond her native Oxford and travel to the mysterious north that seems to have such a strong hold on her uncle, Lord Asriel. When opportunity presents itself in the form of a stunning woman and necessity comes in the form of a kidnapped friend, Lyra embarks on a journey that will change her life and make life-long fans of her readers."

—**Alison Morris**, *Wellesley Booksmith,*
Wellesley, MA

"Demanding repeated readings, this is a full and rich fantasy novel that becomes a first step in a journey through faith, love, and life itself. It's beautifully written and fun to boot. I catch myself gasping with surprise and true suspense."

—**Jean Westcott**, *Olsson's Books & Records,*
Arlington, VA

THE HOBBIT

BY J. R. R. TOLKIEN

"Tolkien's admirable body of work introduced generations of readers to fantasy. Many of those readers started with the story of the unassuming Bilbo Baggins, Hobbit of the Shire. In *The Hobbit*, Bilbo has an unexpected party with a wizard and thirteen dwarves, travels across half of Middle Earth, befriends elves and giant eagles, clashes with trolls and goblins and wolves (oh, my), finds a magic ring, and has a battle of wits with a dragon under the mountain. There and back again, our small hero handles a very hazardous situation with aplomb, while hardly ever missing a meal."
—Patrick Heffernan and Maryelizabeth Hart, *Mysterious Galaxy,*
San Diego, CA

"The extensively researched and updated edition of *The Annotated Hobbit*, by Tolkien scholar and independent bookseller Douglas A. Anderson, includes incredibly detailed notations as well as excerpts and illustrations from numerous foreign translations of this classic fantasy tale. A fascinating read and an excellent choice for Tolkien collectors."
—Heather M. Fierst, *The Book Bag,*
Valparaiso, IN

THE LION, THE WITCH, AND THE WARDROBE

⚘ BY C.S. LEWIS

"I can clearly recall the day in fourth grade when I checked *The Lion, the Witch, and the Wardrobe* out of the library and entered a new world. *The Lion, the Witch, and the Wardrobe* was the first of the series to be written, and to my mind is still the best. When the four children step through the magic wardrobe into the land of Narnia and meet Mr. Tumnus, the faun, the reader becomes part of an enchanted world, which will last a lifetime."

—**Diane Campbell**, *Paulina Springs Book Company*, Sisters, OR

"This books introduces the possibilities of a parallel universe where siblings could actually work together to fend off evil, mistakes could be forgiven, and the world could have a fresh start. The Pevensie kids literally stumble through an old wardrobe and into a world where they are the long-awaited 'sons of Adam and daughters of Eve' prophesied to save Narnia. They successfully depose the White Witch and put the great lion Aslan back in power. Have you checked the back of your wardrobe lately?"

—**Collette Morgan**, *Wild Rumpus*, Minneapolis, MN

OLIVIA
BY IAN FALCONER

"Olivia, a little pig, is being compared to Eloise. It's apt, but Olivia's certainly a more realistic sketch of many little girls we know (and once were). Perhaps it's that we aspired to be Eloise, but we are Olivia? In any case, she's a delight. Spare illustrations by the famous Falconer and an awfully true-to-life text. Brava, Olivia!"

—from a chorus of voices at *Cody's Books*,
Berkeley, CA

"This is such an endearingly original picture book. In deceptively simple drawings, with splashes of red as the only color, the author has created a piglet to charm the heart of every reader. Most parents will see their child, and most children will see themselves in Olivia. This is very likely another porcine classic."

—**Leslie Reiner**, *Inkwood Books*,
Tampa, FL

THE SISTERHOOD OF THE TRAVELING PANTS

BY ANN BRASHARES

"[This] is a fresh, lively look at the friendship of four young ladies facing one inevitable part of growing up—the possibility of growing apart. The first summer that they all must go their separate ways, and reach for their own grown-up personalities, they determine to keep their friendship at the core of their lives. Poignant, funny, real—this story, with the letters the friends write to each other over the summer, will remind you of all the best parts of being best friends."

—**Marjorie Bowman**, *Davis-Kidd Booksellers,*
Memphis, TN

"The only thing four fifteen-year-old girlfriends have to connect them throughout a long summer apart is a pair of $3.49 thrift store jeans—jeans that miraculously fit each girl perfectly. The magic traveling pants will be sent to each girl twice, in the hopes that the girl wearing the pants will have an incredible adventure, make lasting memories, and remember the power of love and friendship."

—**Nikki Mutch**, *UConn Co-op,*
Storrs, CT

❧ TOP
READING GROUP
RECOMMENDATIONS

NATIONALLY, THE NUMBER OF ACTIVE READING GROUPS OF ALL types has exploded over the last few years, reflecting a renewed sense of community, commitment, and intellectual curiosity. Independent bookstores serve as sponsors and, in many cases, the meeting place for these groups. As a happy result, there is a deep and rich well of proven titles from which to choose for your reading group, whatever your population may be.

The following fifty titles are presented in broad categories—The American Landscape, Stories of Memorable Women, Cultural Perspectives, In a Class by Themselves, and Singular Stories, Singularly Told—to help you choose what might be the next best book for your particular reading group. Each title is recommended by an independent bookseller who is intimately familiar with the book and able to guide you with experience and expertise as you search for that special title that will spur thought and discussion among your members.

*The
American
Landscape*

ALL THE PRETTY HORSES
BY CORMAC MCCARTHY

"In this picturesque coming-of-age novel, John Grady Cole and two companions set off for Mexico from a ranch in Texas. This National Book Award–winner is a masterpiece, a gritty yet evocative western told in pitch-perfect prose; a classic quest story with broad appeal."
—**Polly Moran**, *Dartmouth College Bookstore,*
Hanover, NH

THE AMAZING ADVENTURES OF KAVALIER & CLAY
BY MICHAEL CHABON

"This is the crazy New York story of a comic book empire built by artist Joseph Kavalier and his quick-thinking, deal-making cousin Sam Clay. A fast, funny, and achingly moving novel, and one that won the Pulitzer Prize."
—**Kelly Medici**, *NYU Bookstore,*
New York, NY

ANGLE OF REPOSE
 BY WALLACE STEGNER

The American Landscape

"This book epitomizes the difference in viewpoints in America between East and West 150 years ago. A young New Englander marries a mining engineer and settles in a small town in Colorado. This Pulitzer Prize–winning novel raises age-old questions about how free women are to lead their own lives and what happens to marriage when partners cannot compromise."

—Carla Cohen, *Politics and Prose Books and Coffee,* Washington, DC

COLD MOUNTAIN
 BY CHARLES FRAZIER

"A parallel narrative: Inman is seriously injured at the end of the Civil War and begins a dangerous journey home, and Ada has struggled to learn firsthand how to keep alive on her family farm. A beautifully written love story, with much to discuss."

—Robin Powers, *St. Helens Book Shop,* St. Helens, OR

*The
American
Landscape*

CROSSING TO SAFETY

BY WALLACE STEGNER

"An intense relationship drama where every emotion is earned and every character well-drawn. Stegner reveals enduring truths about marriage and the rewards of long lasting friendships... and yes, exposes the trials of both. One of the great books on love by one of the great American writers."

—Leslie Graham,
A Clean Well-Lighted Place for Books,
San Francisco, CA

THE MASTER BUTCHERS SINGING CLUB

BY LOUISE ERDRICH

"This is an emotionally rich novel about German immigrants and their neighbors in Argus, North Dakota. Book groups will especially enjoy discussing this story, because the moral complexity of the characters set against the backdrop of small-town life leaves the reader with much to think about."

—Lanora Hurley, *Harry W. Schwartz Bookshop,*
Mequon, WI

MIDDLESEX

⭐ BY JEFFREY EUGENIDES

"More than a novel about a girl who becomes a man, *Middlesex* is the story of an American century. It offers everything a book group needs: little-known history that broadens our minds; many complex characters who provoke animated debate; and gender issues that take us into contemporary politics."

—**Marian Nielsen,** *Orinda Books,*
Orinda, CA

MOTHERLESS BROOKLYN

⭐ BY JONATHAN LETHEM

"I loved this book, which won the National Book Critics Circle fiction award. The first-person narration, by an orphan with Tourette's syndrome who grows up to be a small-time gangster, is brilliant—James Joyce meets Elmore Leonard. A gritty, funny, and wonderfully written story."

—**Carole Horne,** *Harvard Book Store,*
Cambridge, MA

*The
American
Landscape*

*The
American
Landscape*

PLAINSONG
BY KENT HARUF

"A seventeen-year-old girl, pregnant and with nowhere else to turn, is persuaded to live with the two old McPheron brothers, bachelors who know far more about cattle than teenage girls. The deceptively 'plain' language and structure of this novel mask its complex view of what we owe, and what we can give, to each other. How the characters' lives are changed and their trajectories beyond the novel's close are questions you'll ponder long after you're finished reading."

—**Russ Lawrence**, *Chapter One Book Store,*
Hamilton, MT

POPULATION: 485
MEETING YOUR NEIGHBORS
ONE SIREN AT A TIME
BY MICHAEL PERRY

"*Population: 485* is a story of place—a smart, fascinating look at life in a rural small town. Volunteer EMT Perry takes the reader from sorrow to laughter, from a fire call to the origins of the fire department, and from life to death. Because he is from the small town he

writes about, he tells his story with an
authenticity that resonates with readers and
may prompt them to take a closer look at the
people in their own communities."

—**Carol Dunn,** *Northwind Book & Fiber,*
Spooner, WI

The
American
Landscape

SNOW FALLING ON CEDARS

BY DAVID GUTERSON

"History, romance, mystery—this has it all. A
huge bestseller a few years back, and great for
reading groups."

—**Connie Shelton,** *The Book Shelf,*
Angel Fire, NM

A THOUSAND ACRES

BY JANE SMILEY

"Shakespeare in the heartland! An Iowa farmer
and family patriarch makes power plays in
family farm transactions, wanders through
church suppers, and casts an enormous
shadow over his daughters' lives."

—**Will Peters,** *Annie Bloom's Books,*
Portland, OR

*Stories of
Memorable
Women*

THE ELEGANT GATHERING OF WHITE SNOWS

✦❧ BY KRIS RADISH

"Both men and women will find many discussion topics in this novel about eight women and their joyous friendship. The women revel in the freedom to walk outside the door and leave responsibility behind for a time, and exemplify the way in which sharing a burden with another can lighten that burden's load."

—**Susan Wasson**, *Bookworks,*
Albuquerque, NM

GIRL IN HYACINTH BLUE

✦❧ BY SUSAN VREELAND

"That good things do come in small packages is an understatement in this case. The whole package makes this novel as precious to each reader as the novel's main character, the painting called *The Girl in Hyacinth Blue*, was to each owner. When I finished reading it, I wanted to reread the book back to front."

—**Mary Gay Shipley**,
That Bookstore in Blytheville, Blytheville, AR

GIRL WITH A PEARL EARRING

BY TRACY CHEVALIER

Stories of Memorable Women

"A young servant is asked to model for Vermeer against the wishes of the artist's wife and family. You'll find intrigue, jealousy, and an extraordinary look into the life and work of the artist from the young woman's point of view."

—**Donna DeLacy**, *Portrait of a Bookstore,* Studio City, CA

THE HOURS

BY MICHAEL CUNNINGHAM

"This Pulitzer Prize–winning novel makes brilliant use of Virginia Woolf's *Mrs. Dalloway* to interpolate the stories of three women—two set in contemporary America, the third that of Woolf herself. Beautifully written and totally engaging, we watch as the characters' lives come together and illuminate each other. It's no wonder that *The Hours* is a book group favorite."

—**Karl Kilian**, *Brazos Bookshop,* Houston, TX

Stories of Memorable Women

THE LAST GIRLS
🐾 BY LEE SMITH

"More than thirty years ago, five college roommates traveled, on a lark, down the Mississippi on a makeshift raft. Now, four of them make the trip on a cruise ship, reunited to scatter the ashes of Baby, their wild, beautiful, complicated friend. The reader grows to care about these friends and their choices, which offer rich topics for discussion."
—**Ellen Davis**, *Dragonwings Bookstore,*
Waupaca, WI

MEMOIRS OF A GEISHA
🐾 BY ARTHUR GOLDEN

"Book groups will enjoy discussing the gender issues, including that the author is a man and an American and the story is told in the voice of a famous geisha. Golden convincingly portrays this exotic, mysterious side of twentieth-century Japan."
—**Margie Skinner**,
Book House of Stuyvesant Plaza,
Albany, NY

MRS. KIMBLE

BY JENNIFER HAIGH

Stories of Memorable Women

"I love to begin a book without first reading the jacket copy... especially one like this, where I managed to get well into the book before realizing exactly what was going on. The character of each of the three Mrs. Kimbles is beautifully developed—and through these women, we learn about Mr. Kimble. What a great book club book!"

—Liz Murphy, *Learned Owl Book Shop,*
Hudson, OH

ONE THOUSAND WHITE WOMEN
THE JOURNALS OF MAY DODD

BY JIM FERGUS

"A truly original and imaginative adventure of the women chosen by the U.S. government to be given in the name of peace, and at the suggestion of Chief Little Wolf, as wives to the Cheyenne Indians."

—Nell Hanley, *Armchair Bookstore,*
Dennis, MA

*Stories of
Memorable
Women*

POPE JOAN
BY DONNA CROSS

"The Catholic Church denies (and/or has covered up) the existence of Pope Joan, so this book is a work of literary historical fiction. Whether or not you believe her story, you'll be enthralled by Pope Joan. It's all here: war, romance, Vatican intrigue, politics, and a shocking ending. Rich in discussion topics, *Pope Joan* continues to be a perennial favorite of our book clubs."

—**Kate Larson**, *Book Passage,*
Corte Madera, CA

WILD SWANS
THREE DAUGHTERS OF CHINA
BY JUNG CHANG

"This is the gripping true story of three generations of strong women during the changes and upheavals of life in twentieth-century China."

—**Terry Dallas**, *Armchair Books,*
Pendleton, OR

BALZAC AND THE LITTLE CHINESE SEAMSTRESS

BY DAI SIJIE

Cultural Perspectives

"An amazing narrative about the secret power of literature in the lives of two young Chinese boys who are exiled to a remote mountain village. This is a story as finely detailed as the garments sewn by the little Chinese seamstress with whom the boys fall in love."
—Heather Folan, *Bristol Books, Inc.,* Wilmington, NC

FUGITIVE PIECES

BY ANNE MICHAELS

"Rich with the language of nature, history, and art, this is about a seven-year-old boy who escapes from war-torn Poland, is adopted and nurtured by a Greek geologist, and eventually comes to terms with his past. This book leads to rich discussions about loss, memory, and redemption."
—Virginia Valentine, *Tattered Cover Book Store,* Denver, CO

*Cultural
Perspectives*

THE GOD OF
SMALL THINGS

BY ARUNDHATI ROY

"A wonderful first novel, set in India.
Group discussions focus on Roy's complex
interweaving of a seemingly simple story."

—**Wendy Leavins**, *Wild Iris Books*,
Gainesville, FL

HOUSE OF
SAND AND FOG

BY ANDRE DUBUS III

"More than a riveting story of two people—
a formerly wealthy Iranian immigrant and a
troubled young American woman—fighting to
own the same house, it is also a story of the
clash of two cultures. It's an especially relevant
book for discussion today, providing readers
with insights into both the Muslim and
American mind-sets."

—**Jeanne Morris**, *Bethany Beach Books*,
Bethany Beach, DE

THE HOUSE OF
THE SPIRITS
BY ISABEL ALLENDE

"Beauties with green hair and children who
move saltshakers without touching them mix
with the overthrow of Chile's first democracy
and three generations of aristocracy and rebels.
You want to linger over sentences and turn pages
as fast as you can to find out what happens."
—**Susan Blackwell Ramsey,** *Athena Book Shop,*
Kalamazoo, MI

THE NAMESAKE
BY JHUMPA LAHIRI

"A moving and poignant portrait of a family
in search of self-acceptance and cultural
identity from an author who is a master at
depicting the immigrant experience. No detail
is too small, no character undefined. The result
is a book you can't put down, and reading
groups of all ages, genders, and backgrounds
will find much to discuss."
—**Hester Jeswald,** *Sarasota News & Books,*
Sarasota, FL

Cultural
Perspectives

*Cultural
Perspectives*

READING LOLITA IN TEHRAN
A MEMOIR IN BOOKS
 BY AZAR NAFISI

"This memoir about secretly teaching Western literature to a small group of young women in revolutionary Iran is structured around the novels studied; each section reveals both the transformative powers of literature and the tragic consequences of repression. The author's experience of two cultures colliding provides a wealth of ideas for reading groups to explore."

—**Tripp Ryder**, *Carleton College Bookstore*,
Northfield, MN

THE SHIPPING NEWS
BY ANNIE PROULX

"Proulx transports us with her rich, detailed prose and quirky characters to the icy terrain of Newfoundland."

—**Cheryl McKeon**, *Third Place Books*,
Lake Forest Park, WA

THE SPIRIT CATCHES YOU AND YOU FALL DOWN

∾ BY ANNE FADIMAN

Cultural Perspectives

"A fascinating look at what happens when Western medicine clashes with the cultural practices of America's immigrant Hmong people. This book makes for great discussions about ethical dilemmas."

—Lyn Roberts, *Square Books*, Oxford, MS

THE STONE DIARIES

∾ BY CAROL SHIELDS

"A perfectly ordinary life told in an extraordinary way. Shields uses letters, newspaper clippings, recipes, and other ephemera to spin out the story of Daisy Goodwill, a Manitoba woman born in 1905."

—Peggy Latkovich, *Mac's Backs Paperbacks*, Cleveland Heights, OH

*Cultural
Perspectives*

THEIR EYES WERE WATCHING GOD

BY ZORA NEALE HURSTON

"Hurston's best-known and most controversial novel is about Janie Crawford, a thrice-married spitfire of a woman living in a small Florida town. The fine citizens sit rather comfortably in judgment, ready to render their verdict on Janie's life, but she feels absolutely no compulsion to justify her actions to them."

—**Robin Green-Cary,** *Sibanye,*
Baltimore, MD

WHITE TEETH

BY ZADIE SMITH

"A brilliant debut from a young writer with an uncanny knack for dialogue and description. Cockney Archie and Bengali Samad become lifelong friends after serving together in WWII, and the tragicomic tale of their families weaves themes of fate and free will, race, religion, and assimilation into plot lines involving mutant mice, radical vegetarians, and more."

—**Carla Jimenez,** *Inkwood Books,*
Tampa, FL

BEE SEASON
BY MYLA GOLDBERG

"Book groups will have plenty to discuss
after reading this book, which combines a
dysfunctional family with the mysticism of
the Kabbalah and the intensity of the spelling
bee circuit."

> —Terry Lucas, *Open Book,*
> Westhampton, NY

*In a
Class By
Themselves*

A CONFEDERACY
OF DUNCES
BY JOHN KENNEDY TOOLE

"Ignatius J. Reilly is an overly intelligent,
obese, and more than eccentric recluse whose
few excursions out from his bedroom and into
the real world serve as a catalyst for the
comedy that ensues. This novel will prompt
discussions about the complex character
motivations and relationships and the author's
real-life suicide in 1969."

> —Kyle McAfee, *Fact & Fiction,*
> Missoula MT

*In a
Class By
Themselves*

THE CURIOUS INCIDENT OF THE DOG IN THE NIGHT-TIME

BY MARK HADDON

"An exceptionally bright but socially inept fifteen-year-old is accused of killing the neighbor's dog. He decides to investigate the crime. The novel delves into the minds of autistic children and will lead to frank discussion about how others view the world."

—**Valerie Koehler,** *Blue Willow Bookshop,*
Houston, TX

THE EYRE AFFAIR

BY JASPER FFORDE

"Imagine being able to jump inside your favorite book and watch the plot unfold before your eyes. In *The Eyre Affair,* heroine Thursday Next finds herself in all sorts of trouble in her work and love life. Reading groups will enjoy this funny, fast-paced—even dizzying, at times—story of time travel and adventure."

—**Jennifer Roberts,** *Wind & Tide Bookshop,*
Oak Harbor, WA

THE HUMAN STAIN

❧ BY PHILIP ROTH

"Roth's book is the third in his series of chronicles of otherwise honorable lives destroyed by 'the indigenous American berserk.' Professor Coleman Silk, exiled from his job on accusations of racism, is forced to contemplate the conduct of his life and career, with results both purifying and dangerous. Gripping stuff."

—Sacha Arnold, *Bookshop Santa Cruz,* Santa Cruz, CA

In a Class By Themselves

THE SPARROW

❧ BY MARY DORIA RUSSELL

"When music emanates from a distant planet, a gifted linguist and a not-so-spiritual Jesuit priest assemble a crew for a space expedition. This novel will consistently intrigue devotees of science fiction, as well as those who don't usually read books in this genre because of the way in which it addresses both spiritual questions, and the unintended consequences of exploring new worlds."

—Cammie Mannino, *Halfway Down the Stairs,* Rochester, MI

*In a
Class By
Themselves*

THE TIME TRAVELER'S WIFE
BY AUDREY NIFFENEGGER

"Due to a genetic disorder, Henry finds himself spontaneously displaced in time to moments in his past and future, many of which involve the love of his life, Clare. Book groups will discover the connections between these two soul mates through a patchwork of scenes and settings that ultimately connect into one poignant history."

—**Tom Heywood**, *The Babbling Book*,
Haines, AK

WICKED
THE LIFE AND TIMES OF THE WICKED WITCH OF THE WEST
BY GREGORY MAGUIRE

"Maguire tells this familiar story from the point of view of the Wicked Witch of the West. In the process, he gives us a fascinating look at being an outsider and the nature of good and evil, and reminds us that the winner of any conflict is the one who gets to tell the story."

—**Peggy Hailey**, *BookPeople*,
Austin, TX

THE CRIMSON PETAL AND THE WHITE

🐾 BY MICHEL FABER

Singular Stories Singularly Told

"Faber presents us with a sprawling Victorian novel, told with all the typical devices and designs, yet turning the genre on its ear. Where Dickens turned a blind eye, Faber shares every shocking detail of 1800s London. The trials of the wealthy Rackham family make for an unforgettable story."

—**Drew Phillips**, *Warwick's*, La Jolla, CA

EVERYTHING IS ILLUMINATED

🐾 BY JONATHAN SAFRAN FOER

"More than one English language is at work in Foer's absolutely captivating book. This book's riches (and they are many) lie in its astonishing range of humor and horror, an awareness of past and present, and a presence that takes very certain words to say. Say them Foer does: daringly, hauntingly, and deeply."

—**Rick Simonson**, *Elliott Bay Book Company*, Seattle, WA

*Singular
Stories
Singularly
Told*

GEEK LOVE
BY KATHERINE DUNN

"A carney couple deliberately has a brood of circus freaks. To debate: the dark and wild characters, the author's humor and writing style, and the cultural standards of freakishness and beauty!"

—**Pam Harcourt**, *Women & Children First,*
Chicago, IL

THE MIRACLE LIFE OF EDGAR MINT
BY BRADY UDALL

"From the moment the mailman runs over his head, this kid grabs your attention and your heart and doesn't let go. Edgar takes everything that life has to throw at him, teaches us about good and evil, and, in the end, finds his own place in the world. Is he admirable, pathetic, or a bit twisted? You decide."

—**Barb Bassett**, *The Red Balloon Bookshop,*
St. Paul, MN

THE NO. I LADIES' DETECTIVE AGENCY

*BY ALEXANDER MCCALL SMITH

"When the middle-aged Botswanan Mma Ramotswe inherits some money, she renovates an office, borrows a typewriter, and hires a secretary. What more do you need to open the number-one Ladies' Detective Agency? This is the first in a series of surprising, insightful, and charming mysteries."

—Amy Rosenfield, *Joseph-Beth Booksellers,* Cleveland, OH

Singular Stories Singularly Told

THE PROFESSOR AND THE MADMAN

A TALE OF MURDER AND THE MAKING OF THE OXFORD ENGLISH DICTIONARY

*BY SIMON WINCHESTER

"This true story begins like a gothic murder mystery and then takes you on a fascinating journey exploring the making of the Oxford English Dictionary."

—Susie Fruncillo, *Lake Country Booksellers,* White Bear Lake, MN

*Singular
Stories
Singularly
Told*

RUNNING WITH SCISSORS
A MEMOIR
BY AUGUSTEN BURROUGHS

"Burroughs' story will bring you to your knees, whether laughing or crying at the extremes of his childhood. A discussion of this book will surely be lively and heartfelt... and will go on all night."

—**Martha Wales**, *Bear Pond Books of Montpelier*, Montpelier, VT

THREE JUNES
BY JULIA GLASS

"Glass has created a novel full of wisdom and interesting observations on life. The author is adept at intertwining and examining the lives of the various characters, their loves, and their relationships. There's a lot to digest in this great book club selection."

—**Marianne Kitchell**, *Madison Park Books*, Seattle, WA

❧ TOP CLASSICS
FOR CHILDREN AND
YOUNG ADULTS

FOR GENERATIONS, PARENTS AND GRANDPARENTS HAVE BEEN concerned about their children's reading tastes and habits. The current proliferation of competing media has only served to heighten and focus that concern.

Book Sense booksellers have provided knowledgeable alternatives with exciting and engaging reading recommendations in various age categories, guaranteed to provide hours of pleasure and challenge for all readers.

The following fifty titles are those most highly favored to begin the list of new standards, conveniently divided into different age ranges, including toddlers and preschoolers (ages 1–3), beginning readers (4–8), middle readers (9-12), and young adults. Independent booksellers welcome your inquiries, and are ready and willing to help you build the very best library for your children and grandchildren.

*For
Toddlers &
Pre-Schoolers
(Ages 1–3)*

BARK, GEORGE

BY JULES FEIFFER

"When read aloud, this sweet little story
never fails to elicit chortles, guffaws, and
belly laughs. Children will find this little dog
hilarious when asked to bark by his mom but
instead... well, you'll see. The surprise ending
will amuse adults as well."

—**Trudy Barash**, *Canterbury Booksellers*,
Madison, WI

DIARY OF A WOMBAT

BY JACKIE FRENCH
ILLUSTRATED BY BRUCE WHATLEY

"Jackie French is one of my favorite discoveries.
In this hilarious picture book, she teams up
with Bruce Whatley, who perfectly illustrates
a day in the life of your friendly neighborhood
wombat. Two incredible talents combine to
make this one of my favorite new children's
books!"

—**Beth Henkes**, *University Book Store*,
Bellevue, WA

DON'T TAKE YOUR SNAKE FOR A STROLL

BY KARIN IRELAND
ILLUSTRATED BY DAVID CATROW

"This is an immensely readable book with exuberant illustrations. It's hard to resist the snake on a downtown stroll, frogs loose in a gourmet restaurant, and an elephant sunning itself at the beach."

—**Carol Dunn**, *Northwind Book & Fiber,*
Spooner, WI

*For
Toddlers &
Pre-Schoolers
(Ages 1–3)*

GASPARD AND LISA FRIENDS FOREVER

BY ANNE GUTMAN
ILLUSTRATED BY GEORG HALLENSLEBEN

"The Gaspard and Lisa books are a complete delight—funny, exciting, and teaching interesting lessons. And I absolutely adore the illustrations, which are bright, cute, and certainly age-appropriate to the text. I can't say enough about them. To me, they're just perfect, some of my very favorite books."

—**Carrie Graves**, *The Happy Bookseller,*
Columbia, SC

For
Toddlers &
Pre-Schoolers
(Ages 1–3)

HOW I BECAME A PIRATE
BY MELINDA LONG
ILLUSTRATED BY DAVID SHANNON

"A witty tale that pirates of all ages will enjoy. Readers will not be able to resist jumping into pirate-speak as they enjoy the catchy rhyming verse and the bold and colorful illustrations."
—Lisa Fabiano, *Hearts & Stars Bookshop,*
Canton, MA

SLEEPY BEARS
BY MEM FOX
ILLUSTRATED BY KERRY ARGENT

"A great new bedtime read, and the pictures are delightful."
— Jane Stroh, *The Bookstore,*
Glen Ellyn, IL

SNOW MUSIC

BY LYNNE RAE PERKINS

"What does winter sound like? In this artful, deceptively simple picture book, Lynne Rae Perkins has captured the oft-missed harmonies of a season—from the rumbling chorus of a passing snowplow to the 'jingle, huff, jingle, huff' of a dog trotting through the snow."

—Alison Morris, *Wellesley Booksmith,*
Wellesley, MA

*For
Toddlers &
Pre-Schoolers
(Ages 1–3)*

STELLA, FAIRY OF THE FOREST

BY MARIE-LOUISE GAY

"Stella and little brother Sam return in this fantastic new adventure. Sam has never seen a fairy, so he and Stella set off for the forest in search of some and learn many things along the way. This is a great choice for story time; it's one you won't mind reading over and over."

—Mary Kooyman, *Scott's Bookstore,*
Mount Vernon, WA

*For
Toddlers &
Pre-Schoolers
(Ages 1–3)*

TOO BIG!

BY CLAIRE MASUREL

ILLUSTRATED BY HANAKO WAKIYAMA

"This is my two-year-old nephew's favorite book! Charlie wins a giant (and I mean giant) stuffed animal at the fair. A playful, colorful, and kind book."

—**Andrea Sandke**, *Kepler's Books and Magazines*, Menlo Park, CA

TRAFFIC JAM

A FOLD-OUT BOOK

BY NORMAN YOUNG AND ANDY CRAWFORD

"The book folds out to reveal a slow-moving tractor and the cars lined up behind, letting us visualize the futility of the characters' impatience, but it encourages the laid-back attitude of the 'groovy pop star': 'chill out, man, it's okay.'"

—**Mary Brice**, *Tattered Cover Book Store*, Denver, CO

THE TREE

BY DANA LYONS
ILLUSTRATED BY DAVID DANIOTH

For Toddlers & Pre-Schoolers (Ages 1–3)

"The illustrations are beautiful, the text is simple, and the message clear: It is our place to protect our natural resources. This book is very beautiful and moving."

—Julie Heidtman, *Page One Bookstore,* Albuquerque, NM

WOOLEYCAT'S MUSICAL THEATER (BOOK WITH AUDIO CD)

BY DENNIS HYSOM
ILLUSTRATED BY CHRISTINE WALKER

"The text and lyrics consist of cleverly fractured Mother Goose rhymes that add up to a ten-song musical. The illustrations are adorable, and the musical accompaniment is sprightly and beautifully produced."

—Lilla Weinberger, *Readers' Books,* Sonoma, CA

*For
Beginning
Readers
(Ages 4–8)*

THE DINOSAURS OF WATERHOUSE HAWKINS

BY BARBARA KERLEY
ILLUSTRATED BY BRIAN SELZNICK

"This is a really fun and endearing true story about the man who made the first life-size models of dinosaurs back in the mid-1800s. Waterhouse Hawkins was part scientist/part artist. He was inspired to do something that few thought he could, and his story has a very bittersweet ending. The illustrations are beautiful and the story is one few know, even we adults."
—**Stephen Hammill**, *Inkwood Books*, Tampa, FL

A FINE, FINE SCHOOL

BY SHARON CREECH
ILLUSTRATED BY HARRY BLISS

"A proud principal thinks his school is so fine, it should be open every day! Tillie then visits his office and tells him that other kinds of learning need to occur. A delightful, funny cautionary tale."
—**Karen Miller**, *Anderson's Book Shop*, Naperville, IL

GOBBLE, QUACK, MOON

BY MATTHEW GOLLUB

ILLUSTRATED BY JUDY LOVE

For Beginning Readers (Ages 4–8)

"*Gobble, Quack, Moon* is a wacky, far out-in-space tale set in rhyming verse and accompanied by a CD of music and the author reading the story to musical accompaniment. Farm animal friends become bored with life with Farmer Beth and decide to perform a ballet on the moon."

—**Bob Spear,** *The Book Barn,*
Leavenworth, KS

GRANDPA'S CORNER STORE

BY DYANNE DISALVO-RYAN

"A tribute to independently owned community businesses. Lucy's grandpa's corner grocery store is a vital part of the neighborhood. Grandpa knows every customer and what they need. A huge supermarket opens up nearby and Lucy's grandpa fears he may have to shut down, but the community pulls together to support the store."

—**Dana Harper,** *Brystone Children's Books,*
Watauga, TX

For Beginning Readers (Ages 4–8)

IF THE WORLD WERE A VILLAGE
A BOOK ABOUT THE WORLD'S PEOPLE
BY DAVID J. SMITH
ILLUSTRATED BY SHELAGH ARMSTRONG

"This book is so cool! If the world consisted of one-hundred people in one small village, how many of those people would have computers? Have enough to eat? Be able to read? Smith makes global issues accessible to all. Perfect to introduce children to the world around them."
—**Nikki Mutch**, *UConn Co-op*, Storrs, CT

M IS FOR MAJESTIC
A NATIONAL PARKS ALPHABET
BY DAVID DOMENICONI
ILLUSTRATED BY PAM CARROL

"This is a wonderful addition to Sleeping Bear Press' alphabet series. Great rhyming text for little ones and detail boxes for older children— plus large colorful illustrations—bring learning about America's national treasures to life."
—**Lisa Fabiano**, *Hearts & Stars Bookshop*, Canton, MA

OLD TURTLE AND THE BROKEN TRUTH

BY DOUGLAS WOOD
ILLUSTRATED BY JON J. MUTH

For Beginning Readers (Ages 4–8)

"Douglas Wood's stirring and eloquent fable, soulfully illustrated by Jon J. Muth's luminous watercolors, offers readers of all ages inspiration, hope, and a healing vision of peace. I don't know when I have been so touched and thrilled over a book."

—**Virginia Hobson Hicks**, *Books on the Bluff,*
Townsend, GA

THE QUILTMAKER'S GIFT

BY JEFF BRUMBEAU
ILLUSTRATED BY GAIL DE MARCKEN

"This is the most beautiful children's book I've seen in a long time. The story about a greedy king and the true meaning of wealth is wonderful and the illustrations are exquisite. It is incredible how many different things one sees each time a page is turned."

—**Susan Wasson**, *Bookworks,*
Albuquerque, NM

For Beginning Readers (Ages 4–8)

TAKE ME OUT OF THE BATHTUB
AND OTHER SILLY DILLY SONGS
BY ALAN KATZ
ILLUSTRATED BY DAVID CATROW

"My co-workers and I have hardly been able to conduct business lately. We have been lying on the floor convulsive while singing the songs in the book. The illustrations by Catrow are absolutely wonderful."

—**Alicia Greis**, *Colorado College Bookstore*, Colorado Springs, CO

TOOT & PUDDLE
TOP OF THE WORLD
BY HOLLY HOBBIE

"Fans of Toot and Puddle rejoice! The latest whimsical adventure is here. Toot takes a walk that turns into a trip to France and Nepal, and Puddle sets off to find him. Adults will love it, too!"

—**Jenne Herbst**, *Quail Ridge Books & Music*, Raleigh, NC

THE WATER HOLE

BY GRAEME BASE

For
Beginning
Readers
(Ages 4–8)

"Here is a treasure of a book to come back to again and again. With each reading, I find more details in these stunning illustrations which surprise and delight in this story of a disappearing water hole. This multi-layered creation combines counting and hidden pictures, geography and zoology, an important environmental lesson, and exquisitely detailed art."

—**Mari Enoch**, *The Bookloft*, Great Barrington, MA

YOU READ TO ME *&* I'LL READ TO YOU

20TH-CENTURY STORIES TO SHARE

BY JANET SCHULMAN

"What a joy! A true treasure that not only includes *No Kiss for Mother* but also *Flat Stanley* with the original illustrations by Tomi Ungerer. So many great stories, and a tremendous value to boot!"

—**Amy Nina Baum**, *Red Balloon Bookshop*, St. Paul, MN

*For
Middle
Readers
(Ages 9–12)*

BUD, NOT BUDDY

BY CHRISTOPHER PAUL CURTIS

"In Bud, an orphaned ten-year-old black boy trying to survive in the Depression, Curtis has written the most endearing character I've encountered in a long time. Written with grace and gentleness."

— **Nicky Salan**, *Cover to Cover Booksellers,* San Francisco, CA

THE CONCH BEARER

BY CHITRA BANERJEE DIVAKARUNI

"An unlikely group wends its way across India from Kolkata to the great Himalayas, in a race against time to save themselves and all of mankind from evil and destruction. A first-rate fantasy with valuable lessons about friendship, family, and loyalty."

—**Sarah Parker,** *Scott's Bookstore,* Mount Vernon, WA

GRANNY TORRELLI MAKES SOUP

BY SHARON CREECH

"This may be master storyteller and
Newbery Medal-winner Sharon Creech's
finest offering to young readers yet. Over
zesty Italian cooking, Granny Torrelli offers
insight to Rosie by telling tales of her own
childhood friend Pedro. It is simple wisdom
told with brilliant charm."

—**Mary Brice**, *Tattered Cover Book Store,*
Denver, CO

*For
Middle
Readers
(Ages 9–12)*

A HOUSE CALLED AWFUL END: BOOK ONE OF THE EDDIE DICKENS TRILOGY

BY PHILIP ARDAGH
ILLUSTRATED BY DAVID ROBERTS

"All you fans of Mr. Snicket and Mr. Dahl,
here you go! Mr. Ardagh is here with a new
series about kids persevering despite some dire
straits. Here's the first ridiculous, witty, and
fun installment. Enjoy!"

—**Carol Schweppe**, *Hicklebee's,*
San Jose, CA

For Middle Readers (Ages 9–12)

INKHEART
BY CORNELIA FUNKE

"*Inkheart* is a wonderfully told fairy tale and adventure that will be enjoyed by both young and old alike. Cornelia Funke is a remarkable storyteller, who holds you spellbound until you've read every word. I will be treasuring and handing this story down to my children and, I hope, to their children one day."

—Lee Musgjerd, *Lee's Book Emporium,*
Glasgow, MT

LOSER
BY JERRY SPINELLI

"This was riveting from the very first page. This book is written for middle readers and teens, but I *highly* recommend this to any parent, and especially one who has a son. It had me laughing and crying. This book cuts to the core of what it is like to be a thoughtful and sensitive young man in our sometimes cruel and confusing world. This is one of the best books I have read in years."

—Tom Montan, *Copperfield's Books,*
Sebastopol, CA

LOVE THAT DOG
BY SHARON CREECH

"Inspired by author Walter Dean Myers
and encouraged by his teacher, young Jack
tries to describe, through a series of poetry
assignments, the life and loss of his beloved
yellow dog. Creech's story is spare, touching,
and very fine."

—Ellen Davis, *Dragonwings Bookstore*,
Waupaca, WI

*For
Middle
Readers
(Ages 9–12)*

THE MISFITS
BY JAMES HOWE

"With humor and sensitivity, Howe explores
the issues of name-calling, fitting in, and
standing up for what's right. Young readers
will appreciate the lesson that youthful
rebellion is not always a bad thing."

—Eric Robbins, *Apple Valley Books*,
Winthrop, ME

PICTURES OF HOLLIS WOODS

BY PATRICIA REILLY GIFF

"Twelve-year-old Hollis Woods is an artistic, determined foster kid. Giff paints a picture of her troubled past and current struggle to find a family rich with feeling, life, and characters. Her ability to draw the reader into her tender writing never failed to thrill me, both as a bookseller and a reader."

—**Jonatha Foli**, *Copperfield's Books*,
Sebastopol, CA

SAHARA SPECIAL

BY ESMÉ RAJI CODELL

"Sahara is a gifted writer trapped in a lonely, troubled ten-year-old. A brilliant, compassionate, eccentric teacher and a determined, supportive mom help her unlock her gifts. For fans of Codell's *Educating Esmé*, the news is great: Her first novel is an exuberant success."

—**Banna Rubinow**, *The River's End Bookstore*,
Oswego, NY

THE SEEING STONE

BY KEVIN CROSSLEY-HOLLAND

For Middle Readers (Ages 9–12)

"While many writers have tried their hands at the Arthurian saga, this author has truly brought it to life. He combines humor with rich prose and scholarship, with characters you care about. Here is the first in a trilogy that will, like Harry Potter, be enjoyed by readers of all ages."

—**Rita Moran**, *Apple Valley Books,*
Winthrop, ME

THE TALE OF DESPEREAUX

BY KATE DICAMILLO

ILLUSTRATED BY TIMOTHY B. ERING

"Despereaux, a tiny mouse with unusually large ears, has broken the most serious law of mousedom by speaking to the princess. He is consequently sentenced to spend the rest of his days in the dungeon with evil no-good rats. Hard to resist this fun adventure!"

—**Natacha Maria Pouech**,
Bear Pond Books of Montpelier,
Montpelier, VT

WITNESS

 BY KAREN HESSE

"A remarkable book, written in poetic form using eleven different voices, telling of the effect of the Ku Klux Klan on a 1924 Vermont community. Suspenseful, scary, yet often funny and thrilling, it is the saga of ordinary people in extraordinary circumstances. How they then react and survive is both tragic and heroic. A wonderful new novel from Hesse."

—**Marge Grutzmacher**, *Passtimes Books,* Sister Bay, WI

ABHORSEN
BY GARTH NIX

"I haven't been as excited about a sequel (following *Sabriel* and *Lirael*) since *The Amber Spyglass!* Nix reveals a world heading towards the ultimate battle between good and evil, but his characters and the magic that they wield are powerful and unique."
　　—Tracy Wynne, *Cover To Cover Booksellers*,
　　　　　　　　　San Francisco, CA

THE AMULET OF SAMARKAND
THE BARTIMAEUS TRILOGY
BOOK I
BY JONATHAN STROUD

"A superb magical adventure story. The book tells the tale of Nathaniel, an ambitious teenage magician whose thirst to avenge an insult from a much more powerful mage leads to a harrowing crisis. This is a funny, tense, elegantly written fantasy adventure, highly recommended."
　　—Dennis Fitzgerald, *All for Kids Books & Music*,
　　　　　　　　　Seattle, WA

For Young Adult Readers

ANGUS, THONGS AND FULL-FRONTAL SNOGGING
CONFESSIONS OF GEORGIA NICOLSON
BY LOUISE RENNISON

"What if Judy Blume and Helen Fielding morphed and wrote a book? This is a hilarious and brazenly honest account of the very complicated world that is the life of a fourteen-year-old London girl."

—Danielle Morgan, *Village Books*, Bellingham, WA

ARTEMIS FOWL
THE ETERNITY CODE, BOOK THREE
EOIN COLFER

"In the latest of the *Artemis Fowl* series, Colfer plays with tone beautifully, maintaining the feeling of a noir adventure series and, bringing the series full-circle, perhaps anticipating further Fowl feats."

—Ben Gibbs, *Book People*, Austin, TX

BUDDHA BOY

BY KATHE KOJA

"Once again, Koja writes about the struggle of young people dealing with anger, as a way of introducing Buddhism. This novel is gritty, realistic, and accessible."
—Carol Schweppe, *Hicklebee's*,
San Jose, CA

For Young Adult Readers

A CORNER OF THE UNIVERSE

BY ANN M. MARTIN

"Based on a secret in the author's own family, this story works on many levels. Martin opens our eyes to shades of gray, where it's hard to make choices and live with the consequences. A great choice for mother/daughter book clubs."
—Valerie Koehler, *Blue Willow Books*,
Houston, TX

FIRE BRINGER

BY DAVID CLEMENT-DAVIES

"I read this book in a day, then gave it to my thirteen-year-old son, and he read it in a day. We *loved* it!!! Set in ancient Scotland, it's a story with a little mythology, fantasy, and mystery. It reminds me of the *Redwall* series and *Watership Down*, and I've told people here that it's my 'Harry Potter pick' for this year. I enjoyed it that much."

—**Suzanne Droppert**, *Liberty Bay Books*,
Poulsbo, WA

GREEN ANGEL

BY ALICE HOFFMAN

"Hoffman weaves a futuristic tale of near annihilation, taking one gentle, loving teenage girl from a close-knit family and leaving her alone to deal with the loss and distraction of her life and world. This chillingly realistic story is set in a world we might one day know."

—**Roxanne Campbell**, *Sam Weller's Books*,
Salt Lake City, UT

IN MY HANDS
MEMORIES OF A
HOLOCAUST RESCUER
 BY IRENE GUT OPDYKE
WITH JENNIFER ARMSTRONG

For Young Adult Readers

"I've been telling everyone about this powerful book about a young, inspiring heroine. Now that it's in paperback, it's perfect for school reading lists as well as adult reading groups. Please read it!"
—Betsy Detwiler, *Buttonwood Books and Toys,* Cohasset, MA

LEARNING TO SWIM
A MEMOIR
 BY ANN TURNER

"I found this book incredibly moving. It will gently and truthfully tell children and adults what survivors of sexual abuse live through. For the survivors, it will prove to be a shame-lifting step on the path to their own healing."
—Marian Hughes, *Bookshop Santa Cruz,* Santa Cruz, CA

For Young Adult Readers

PIRATES!
BY CELIA REES

"In the form of a memoir, this stunning novel, set in the 1700s, tells the story of two young women who dramatically change the course of their lives. Full of adventure and emotional depth, it's a must-read!"

—**Anna Lund**, *The King's English*, Salt Lake City, UT

TIME STOPS FOR NO MOUSE
BY MICHAEL HOEYE

"I cannot rest until the world knows about this [originally] self-published gem! This is possibly the most delightful book I have ever fondled and perused. The plot might be described as *Wind in the Willows* meets Carl Hiaasen! Hermux, the village watchmaker, is smitten by Linka—adventuress, daredevil, aviatrix, and a fine-looking mouse to boot. When she disappears, the action takes off. I am just so excited about this book. Once people pick it up and begin to read, they cannot resist it."

—**Bobbie Tichenor**, *Annie Bloom's*, Portland, OR

WHALE TALK

BY CHRIS CRUTCHER

For Young Adult Readers

"This is the best novel that I've read in a long, long time. In a war between the jocks and the freaks, T. J. Jones gradually becomes a wise and fair 'Everyman,' representing all that is good in our society. This book should be required reading for every freak, geek, and jock living the American dream/nightmare of high school."

—**Collette Morgan,** *Wild Rumpus Books,* Minneapolis, MN

Appendix

❧ BOOK SENSE "TOP TENS" FROM THE FIRST FIVE YEARS

AS PART OF ITS FIFTH BIRTHDAY CELEBRATION IN 2004, BOOK Sense circulated a ballot with the following 375 titles—all of the top-10-ranked books on the Book Sense Best Books lists over the last five years. More than 1,000 members voted on the adult and children's titles they most enjoyed hand-selling. Their vote resulted in "The Top Picks," which begins on page 1.

Adult Fiction

About the Author, John Colapinto
Absolute Zero, Chuck Logan
Across the Nightingale Floor: Book One of the Tales of the Otori, Lian Hearn
Ahab's Wife or, The Star-Gazer, Sena Jeter Naslund
All Over Creation, Ruth Ozeki
All We Know of Heaven, Remy Rougeau
American Gods, Neil Gaiman
American Woman, Susan Choi
Atonement, Ian McEwan
Ava's Man, Rick Bragg
Balzac and the Little Chinese Seamstress, Dai Sijie
Bee Season, Myla Goldberg
Bel Canto, Ann Patchett

Blackwater Sound, James W. Hall
The Blind Assassin, Margaret Atwood
Blood of Victory, Alan Furst
Blue Diary, Alice Hoffman
The Book of Illusions, Paul Auster
The Bridge, Doug Marlette
Burning Marguerite, Elizabeth Inness-Brown
The Center of Everything, Laura Moriarty
Chalktown, Melinda Haynes
City of Dreams: A Novel of Nieuw Amsterdam and Early Manhattan, Beverly Swerling
City of Light, Lauren Belfer
The Clearing, Tim Gautreaux
Cloud of Sparrows, Takashi Matsuoka
Cool For You, Eileen Myles
The Corrections, Jonathan Franzen

Crescent, Diana Abu-Jaber
The Crimson Petal and the White,
  Michel Faber
Crooked River Burning, Mark
  Winegardner
Crow Lake, Mary Lawson
The Curve of the World, Marcus Stevens
The Da Vinci Code, Dan Brown
Deafening, Frances Itani
The Death of Vishnu, Manil Suri
The Dive From Clausen's Pier,
  Ann Packer
The Dogs of Babel, Carolyn Parkhurst
Due Preparations for the Plague,
  Janette Turner Hospital
Easter Island, Jennifer Vanderbes
Eat Cake, Jeanne Ray
Ella Minnow Pea: A Novel in Letters,
  Mark Dunn
The Emperor of Ocean Park,
  Stephen L. Carter
Empire Falls, Richard Russo
Everything Is Illuminated,
  Jonathan Safran Foer
The Exchange Student, Kate Gilmore
Falling Angels, Tracy Chevalier
Fatal Flaw, William Lashner
Fearless Jones, Walter Mosley
The Feast of Love, Charles Baxter
The Final Confession of Mabel Stark,
  Robert Hough
Five Quarters of the Orange, Joanne
  Harris
*Fluke: Or I Know Why the Winged
  Whale Sings*, Christopher Moore
Forever, Pete Hamill
Fragrant Harbor, John Lanchester
Friendship Cake, Lynne Hinton
The Fruit of Stone, Mark Spragg

The Gardens of Kyoto, Kate Walbert
Getting Mother's Body, Suzan-Lori
  Parks
Girl in Hyacinth Blue, Susan Vreeland
Gob's Grief, Chris Adrian
A Good House, Bonnie Burnard
Goose Music, Richard Horan
The Grand Complication, Allen
  Kurzweil
The Granite Islands, Sarah Stonich
Hearse of a Different Color,
  Tim Cockey
The Heaven of Mercury, Brad Watson
Hell at the Breech, Tom Franklin
Hell's Bottom, Colorado, Laura
  Pritchett
The Hiding Place, Trezza Azzopardi
How to Cook a Tart, Nina Killham
Ignorance, Milan Kundera
In Her Shoes, Jennifer Weiner
In Sunlight, In a Beautiful Garden,
  Kathleen Cambor
In the Country of the Young, Lisa Carey
The Iron Giant, Ted Hughes
The Jazz Bird, Craig Holden
Julie and Romeo, Jeanne Ray
The Keeper's Son, Homer Hickam
Kindred, Octavia Butler
A Kiss from Maddalena, Christopher
  Castellani
The Known World, Edward P. Jones
The Lake of Dead Languages, Carol
  Goodman
The Last Girls, Lee Smith
The Last Noel, Michael Malone
*The Last Report on the Miracles at
  Little No Horse*, Louise Erdrich
Life of Pi, Yann Martel
Little America, Henry Bromell

The Little Friend, Donna Tartt
The Lovely Bones, Alice Sebold
The Lucky Gourd Shop, Joanna
  Catherine Scott
*Lydia Cassatt Reading the Morning
  Paper*, Harriet Scott Chessman
Lying Awake, Mark Salzman
Maisie Dobbs, Jacqueline Winspear
The Mammoth Cheese, Sheri Holman
The Mark of the Angel, Nancy Huston
The Master Butchers Singing Club,
  Louise Erdrich
Me and Orson Welles, Robert Kaplow
Middlesex, Jeffrey Eugenides
The Miracle Life of Edgar Mint, Brady
  Udall
Miss Julia Speaks Her Mind, Ann B.
  Ross
The Monk Downstairs, Tim Farrington
A Month in the Country, J. L. Carr
Moral Hazard, Kate Jennings
Motherless Brooklyn, Jonathan Lethem
Mrs. Kimble, Jennifer Haigh
Music of the Spheres, Elizabeth Redfern
My Dream of You, Nuala O'Faolain
My Life as a Fake, Peter Carey
Mystic River, Dennis Lehane
*The Neal Pollack Anthology of
  American Literature*, Neal Pollack
No Great Mischief, Alistair MacLeod
No Second Chance, Harlan Coben
Old Flames, John Lawton
One Step Behind, Henning Mankell
Orchard, Larry Watson
A Parchment of Leaves, Silas House
The Passion of Artemisia, Susan
  Vreeland
Pattern Recognition, William Gibson
Peace Like A River, Leif Enger

A Perfect Arrangement, Suzanne Berne
Perfect Match, Jodi Picoult
Perma Red, Debra Magpie Earling
The Photograph, Penelope Lively
Plainsong, Kent Haruf
Poachers: Stories, Tom Franklin
*Poetry Speaks: Hear Great Poets Read
  Their Work, from Tennyson to Plath*,
  Elise Paschen and Rebekah Presson
  Mosby, eds.
The Poisonwood Bible, Barbara
  Kingsolver
Popular Music from Vittula, Mikael
  Niemi
The Price of Passion, Evelyn Palfrey
Purple Hibiscus, Chimamanda Ngozi
  Adichie
*Quicksilver: Volume One of the
  Baroque Cycle*, Neal Stephenson
Red Poppies: A Novel of Tibet, Alai
The Red Tent, Anita Diamant
Renato's Luck, Jeff Shapiro
River, Cross My Heart, Breena Clarke
The River King, Alice Hoffman
*Sailing Alone Around the Room: New
  and Selected Poems*, Billy Collins
Samaritan, Richard Price
The Secret Life of Bees, Sue Monk Kidd
Servants of the Map: Stories, Andrea
  Barrett
Shooting Dr. Jack, Norman Green
Shutter Island, Dennis Lehane
Signal & Noise, John Griesemer
Slow Way Home, Michael Morris
The Solace of Leaving Early, Haven
  Kimmel
Sophie and the Rising Sun, Augusta
  Trobaugh
The Sparrow, Mary Doria Russell

Spies, Michael Frayn
Storm Riders, Craig Lesley
Sweet Dream Baby, Sterling Watson
Tell No One, Harlan Coben
That Old Ace in the Hole, Annie Proulx
Train, Pete Dexter
Tropic of Night, Michael Gruber
The True Account: A Novel of the
    Lewis & Clark & Kinneson
    Expeditions, Howard Frank Mosher
Uniform Justice: A Commissario Guido
    Brunetti Mystery, Donna Leon
The Valley of Light, Terry Kay
The Way the Crow Flies, Ann-Marie
    MacDonald
A Week in Winter, Marcia Willett
What I Loved, Siri Hustvedt
When the Elephants Dance, Tess Uriza
    Holthe
White Teeth, Zadie Smith
Winter Range, Claire Davis
Year of Wonders: A Novel of the
    Plague, Geraldine Brooks

Adult Nonfiction

Africana: The Encyclopedia of the
    African and African-American
    Experience, Kwame Anthony Appiah
    and Henry Louis Gates, Jr.
All Souls: A Family Story from Southie,
    Michael Patrick MacDonald
Art at the Turn of the Millennium, Uta
    Grosenick and Burkhard
    Riemschneider, eds.
The Athletic Woman's Sourcebook,
    Janis Graham

Black Mass: The Irish Mob, the FBI,
    and the Devil's Deal, Dick Lehr and
    Gerard O'Neill
The Blood Runs Like a River Through
    My Dreams: A Memoir, Nasdijj
Bookstore: The Life and Times of
    Jeannette Watson and Books & Co.,
    Lynne Tillman
Borrowed Finery: A Memoir, Paula Fox
Brunelleschi's Dome: How a
    Renaissance Genius Reinvented
    Architecture, Ross King
A Clearing in the Distance: Frederick
    Law Olmsted and America in the
    Nineteenth Century, Witold
    Rybczynski
Coal: A Human History, Barbara Freese
Confederacy of Silence: A True Tale of
    the New Old South, Richard Rubin
The Danger Tree: Memory, War, and
    the Search for a Family's Past, David
    MacFarlane
The Devil in the White City: Murder,
    Magic, and Madness at the Fair That
    Changed America, Erik Larson
Don't Let's Go to the Dogs Tonight,
    Alexandra Fuller
Driving Mr. Albert: A Trip Across
    America with Einstein's Brain,
    Michael Paterniti
Fast Food Nation: The Dark Side of the
    All-American Meal, Eric Schlosser
Fruitflesh: Seeds of Inspiration for
    Women Who Write, Gayle Brandeis
A Girl Named Zippy: Growing Up
    Small in Mooreland, Indiana, Haven
    Kimmel
The Good Black: A True Story of Race
    in America, Paul Barrett

Hail to the Chiefs: Presidential Mischief, Morals & Malarkey from George W. to George W., Barbara Holland

Hamlet's Dresser: A Memoir, Bob Smith

Hidden Wisdom: A Guide to the Western Inner Traditions, Richard Smoley and Jay Kinney

Hoop Roots, John Edgar Wideman

In My Hands: Memories of a Holocaust Rescuer, Irene Gut Opdyke with Jennifer Armstrong

Isaac's Storm: A Man, A Time, and the Deadliest Hurricane in History, Erik Larson

Limbo: A Memoir, A. Manette Ansay, Morrow

Living with Books, Alan Powers

Michelangelo and the Pope's Ceiling, Ross King

Mountains Beyond Mountains, Tracy Kidder

My Life in Heavy Metal, Steve Almond

Nickel and Dimed: On (Not) Getting By in America, Barbara Ehrenreich

The Noonday Demon: An Atlas of Depression, Andrew Solomon

Not Fade Away: A Short Life Well Lived, Laurence Shames and Peter Barton

Off to the Side: A Memoir, Jim Harrison

Outsmarting Goliath: How To Achieve Equal Footing with Companies that are Bigger, Richer, Older, and Better Known, Debra Koontz Traverso

Population: 485: Meeting Your Neighbors One Siren at a Time, Michael Perry

The Power of Now, Eckhart Tolle

The Prize Winner of Defiance, Ohio: How My Mother Raised 10 Kids on 25 Words or Less, Terry Ryan

The Quotable Book Lover, Ben Jacobs and Helena Hjalmarsson, eds.

Raising Blaze: Bringing Up an Extraordinary Son in an Ordinary World, Debra Ginsberg

Road Angels: Searching for Home on America's Coast of Dreams, Kent Nerburn

Seabiscuit, Laura Hillenbrand

The Secret Knowledge of Water: Discovering the Essence of the American Desert, Craig Childs

Sixpence House: Lost in a Town of Books, Paul Collins

So Many Books, So Little Time: A Year of Passionate Reading, Sara Nelson

A Soothing Broth: Tonics, Custards, Soups, and Other Cure-Alls for Colds, Coughs, Upset Tummies, and Out-Of-Sorts Days, Pat Willard

Strapless: John Singer Sargent and the Fall of Madame X, Deborah Davis

Sweeping Changes: Discovering the Joy of Zen in Everyday Tasks, Gary Thorp

Sweet Soul Music: Rhythm and Blues and the Southern Dream of Freedom, Peter Guralnick

Take Me With You: A Round-the-World Journey to Invite a Stranger Home, Brad Newsham

Touching My Father's Soul: A Sherpa's Journey to the Top of Everest, Jamling Tenzing Norgay

Utopia Parkway: The Life and Work of Joseph Cornell, Deborah Solomon

Waiting for Snow in Havana: Confessions of a Cuban Boy, Carlos Eire

What the Dormouse Said: Lessons for Grown-Ups from Children's Books, Amy Gash

Without Reservations: The Travels of an Independent Woman, Alice Steinbach

Zen Dog, Toni Tucker and Judith Adler

For Toddlers and Preschoolers (Ages 1–3)

Bark, George, Jules Feiffer

Diary of a Wombat, Jackie French; illustrated by Bruce Whatley

Diary of a Worm, Doreen Cronin; illustrated by Harry Bliss

Don't Take Your Snake for a Stroll, Karin Ireland; illustrated by David Catrow

Gaspard and Lisa Friends Forever, Anne Gutman; illustrated by Georg Hallensleben

How I Became a Pirate, Melinda Long; illustrated by David Shannon

Olivia, Ian Falconer

Olivia Saves the Circus, Ian Falconer

Sleepy Bears, Mem Fox; illustrated by Kerry Argent

Snow Music, Lynne Rae Perkins

Stella, Fairy of the Forest, Marie-Louise Gay

Too Big!, Claire Masurel; illustrated by Hanako Wakiyama

Traffic Jam: A Fold-Out Book, Norman Young and Andy Crawford

The Tree, Dana Lyons; illustrated by David Danioth

Wooleycat's Musical Theater, Dennis Hysom; illustrated by Christine Walker

For Beginning Readers (Ages 4–8)

Amelia and Eleanor Go for a Ride, Pam Munoz Ryan; illustrated by Brian Selznick

Beatrice's Goat, Page McBrier; illustrated by Lori Lohstoeter

BOOK, George Ella Lyon; illustrated by Peter Catalanotto

Dear Mrs. LaRue: Letters from Obedience School, Mark Teague

The Dinosaurs of Waterhouse Hawkins, Barbara Kerley; illustrated by Brian Selznick

Fairy Houses, Tracy Kane

A Fine, Fine School, Sharon Creech; illustrated by Harry Bliss

Fireboat: The Heroic Adventures of the John J. Harvey, Maira Kalman

The Gift, Gabriela Keselman; illustrated by Pep Montserrat

Gobble, Quack, Moon, Matthew Gollub; illustrated by Judy Love

Grandad's Prayers of the Earth, Douglas Wood; illustrated by P. J. Lynch

Grandpa's Corner Store, DyAnne DiSalvo-Ryan

If the World Were a Village: A Book About the World's People, David J. Smith; illustrated by Shelagh Armstrong

The Jazz Fly, Matthew Gollub; illustrated by Karen Hanke

The Lion's Share, Chris Conover

M Is for Majestic: A National Parks Alphabet, David Domeniconi; illustrated by Pam Carroll

Molly Bannaky, Alice McGill; illustrated by Chris K. Soentpiet

New York's Bravest, Mary Pope Osborne; illustrated by Steve Johnson and Lou Fancher

Night Golf, William Miller; illustrated by Cedric Lucas

Old Turtle and the Broken Truth, Douglas Wood; illustrated by Jon J. Muth

The Other Dog, Madeleine L'Engle; illustrated by Christine Davenier

Petite Rouge: A Cajun Red Riding Hood, Mike Artell; illustrated by Jim Harris

Plum: Poems, Tony Mitton; illustrated by Mary GrandPre

Polkabats and Octopus Slacks, Calef Brown

The Quiltmaker's Gift, Jeff Brumbeau; illustrated by Gail de Marcken

Skippyjon Jones, Judy Schachner

The Spider and the Fly, Mary Howitt; illustrated by Tony DiTerlizzi

Stand Tall, Molly Lou Melon, Patty Lovell; illustrated by David Catrow

Stanley's Party, Linda Bailey; illustrated by Bill Slavin

The Starry Night, Neal Waldman

A Story for Bear, Dennis Haseley; illustrated by Jim LaMarche

Take Me Out of the Bathtub and Other Silly Dilly Songs, Alan Katz; illustrated by David Catrow

Ted, Tony DiTerlizzi

Toot & Puddle: Top of the World, Holly Hobbie

The Warlord's Puzzle, Virginia Walton Pilegard; illustrated by Nicolas Debon

The Water Hole, Graeme Base

Weslandia, Paul Fleischman; illustrated by Kevin Hawkes

Wish, Change, Friend, Ian Whybrow; illustrated by Tiphanie Beeke

The Wolves in the Walls, Neil Gaiman; illustrated by Dave McKean

You Read to Me & I'll Read to You, Janet Schulman

For Middle Readers (Ages 9–12)

Arthur: At the Crossing Places, Kevin Crossley-Holland

The Bad Beginning (A Series of Unfortunate Events, Book 1), Lemony Snicket

Because of Winn-Dixie, Kate DiCamillo

Bud, Not Buddy, Christopher Paul Curtis

The Chronicles of Prydain (Series), Lloyd Alexander

The City of Ember, Jeanne DuPrau

The Conch Bearer, Chitra Banerjee Divakaruni

Crispin: The Cross of Lead, Avi

Darby, Jonathan Scott Fuqua

The Dark Is Rising, Susan Cooper

Dave at Night, Gail Carson Levine

Dial-A-Ghost, Eva Ibbotson; illustrated by Kevin Hawkes

Fair Weather, Richard Peck

The Giggler Treatment, Roddy Doyle

Girl in Blue, Ann Rinaldi

Granny Torrelli Makes Soup, Sharon Creech
The Great Good Thing, Roderick Townley
Half Magic, Edward Eager
Harry Potter on Audio (Series), J. K. Rowling, read by Jim Dale
A House Called Awful End: Book One of the Eddie Dickens Trilogy, Philip Ardagh; illustrated by David Roberts
Inkheart, Cornelia Funke
Journey to the River Sea, Eva Ibbotson; illustrated by Kevin Hawkes
The Land, Mildred D. Taylor
The Last Book in the Universe, Rodman Philbrick
Leon and the Spitting Image, Allen Kurzweil; illustrated by Bret Bertholf
The Lion, the Witch, and the Wardrobe, C. S. Lewis
Loser, Jerry Spinelli
Love That Dog, Sharon Creech
Mercedes and the Chocolate Pilot: A True Story of the Berlin Airlift, Margot Theis Raven; illustrated by Gijsbert van Frankenhuyzen
The Misfits, James Howe
Molly Moon's Incredible Book of Hypnotism, Georgia Byng
The Mouse of Amherst, Elizabeth Spires; illustrated by Claire A. Nivola
My Father's Dragon, Ruth Stiles Gannett; illustrated by Ruth Chrisman Gannett
Of Beetles and Angels: A Boy's Remarkable Journey from a Refugee Camp to Harvard, Mawi Asgedom
Olivia Kidney, Ellen Potter; illustrated by Peter H. Reynolds

Pictures of Hollis Woods, Patricia Reilly Giff
Ramona's World, Beverly Cleary
Redwall, Brian Jacques
Regarding the Fountain, Kate Klise
Sahara Special, Esmé Raji Codell
The Sands of Time, Michael Hoeye
The Secrets of Droon (Series), Tony Abbott
The Seeing Stone, Kevin Crossley-Holland
Skellig, David Almond
Slap Your Sides, M. E. Kerr
Stand Tall, Joan Bauer
Stowaway, Karen Hesse
The Tale of Despereaux, Kate DiCamillo; illustrated by Timothy B. Ering
The Thief Lord, Cornelia Funke
The Tiger Rising, Kate DiCamillo
Witness, Karen Hesse
A Wrinkle in Time, Madeleine L'Engle

For Young Adult Readers

Abhorsen, Garth Nix
The Amulet of Samarkand: Bartimaeus Trilogy Book I, Jonathan Stroud
Angus, Thongs and Full-Frontal Snogging: Confessions of Georgia Nicolson, Louise Rennison
Artemis Fowl: The Arctic Incident, Eoin Colfer
Artemis Fowl: The Eternity Code, Eoin Colfer
Big Mouth & Ugly Girl, Joyce Carol Oates
Birdland, Tracy Mack
Buddha Boy, Kathe Koja

Catalyst, Laurie Halse Anderson
Cirque Du Freak: A Living Nightmare, Darren Shan
A Corner of the Universe, Ann M. Martin
Ender's Game, Orson Scott Card
Eragon: Inheritance: Book I, Christopher Paolini
Fault Line, Janet Tashjian
Feed, M. T. Anderson
Fire Bringer, David Clement-Davies
The Folk Keeper, Franny Billingsley
Gingerbread, Rachel Cohn
Girlosophy: A Soul Survival Kit, Anthea Paul
The Golden Compass (His Dark Materials, Book 1), Philip Pullman
Green Angel, Alice Hoffman
The Hobbit, J. R. R. Tolkien
The House of the Scorpion, Nancy Farmer
If There Would Be No Light: Poems from My Heart, Sahara Sunday Spain
In My Hands: Memories of a Holocaust Rescuer, Irene Gut Opdyke with Jennifer Armstrong
Knocked Out by My Nunga-Nungas: Further, Further Confessions of Georgia Nicholson, Louise Rennison

Learning to Swim: A Memoir, Ann Turner
The Life History of a Star, Kelly Easton
Life is Funny, E. R. Frank
Lucy the Giant, Sherri L. Smith
A Northern Light, Jennifer Donnelly
Pirates!, Celia Rees
Rodzina, Karen Cushman
Rules of the Road, Joan Bauer
Sammy Keyes Series, Wendelin Van Draanen
The Second Summer of the Sisterhood, Ann Brashares
The Sisterhood of the Traveling Pants, Ann Brashares
A Step from Heaven, An Na
Straydog, Kathe Koja
Stuck in Neutral, Terry Trueman
Time Stops for No Mouse, Michael Hoeye
True Believer, Virginia Euwer Wolff
The Twelve Gifts of Birth, Charlene Costanzo; photos by Jill Reger, illustrated by Wendy Wassink Ackison
Whale Talk, Chris Crutcher
Witch Child, Celia Rees

Index

Acknowledgments

THIS BOOK WOULD NOT EXIST WITHOUT THE ENTHUSIASTIC participation of those Book Sense booksellers who diligently advise us of those titles that they are confidently recommending to their customers. Their choices form the core of both this volume and of the Book Sense program as a whole, and we are thankful for their continued support.

Gratitude to Esther Margolis, Heidi Sachner, Shannon Berning, Keith Hollaman, Anna Szymanski, Harry Burton, Kevin McGuinness, Paul Sugarman, and the entire staff of Newmarket Press for their generosity, creativity, and genuine care shown at every step of this project, and to Newmarket's trade distributor, W.W. Norton, for their special attention and support. It is especially fitting that our first publishing venture is with two distinguished independent publishers.

Thanks also to the many other publishers, large and small, who have championed the Book Sense program over the past five years. Here's to the next five—and beyond!

Finally, to the staff of the American Booksellers Association, past and present, whose tireless dedication to and promotion of independent bookselling knows no bounds. Rarely have so few accomplished so much and done so with such integrity and professionalism. This book is a testament to their daily labor of love.

About the Authors

BOOK SENSE

A wholly owned subsidiary of the American Booksellers Association, Book Sense, Inc., founded in 1999, administers the Book Sense integrated marketing and branding campaign. Book Sense, comprised of 1,200 bookstore locations in 50 states, seeks to build a national identity for independent bookstores while celebrating the unique character of each store; to create awareness of independent booksellers across the country; and to underscore the collective strength of independent booksellers to consumers. Book Sense includes the Book Sense Picks, the Book Sense Bestseller Lists, a national gift card/certificate program, and BookSense.com. *Book Sense Best Books* is the first book published under its auspices.

THE AMERICAN BOOKSELLERS ASSOCIATION (ABA)

Founded in 1900, the American Booksellers Association (www.bookweb.org) is a not-for-profit trade organization devoted to meeting the needs of its core members—independently owned bookstores with retail storefront locations—through advocacy, education, research, and information dissemination.

Barbara Kingsolver is the author of the novels *The Poisonwood Bible* and *The Bean Trees*, among others, and most recently a collection of essays entitled *Small Wonder*. She is also the founder of the Bellwether Prize, awarded every second year to a novel embodying socially responsible literature, seeking to support "the imagination of human possibilities."

Avin Mark Domnitz, a graduate of the University of Wisconsin and the University of Wisconsin Law School, was an independent bookseller for 18 years with the Harry W. Schwartz Bookshops. Elected to the board of directors of the ABA in 1988, he served as its Treasurer, Vice President, and President before assuming the position of CEO in January 1998.

Mark Nichols was an independent bookseller in various locations from Maine to Connecticut from 1976 through 1993. After seven years in a variety of positions with major publishers, he joined the ABA in 2000, and currently serves as the Director of Book Sense Marketing.